BEYOND ADDICTION
TO AWAKENING

Gary Tzu, PhD

BEYOND ADDICTION TO AWAKENING Originally published as Gray Nixon, The Sun Rises in the Evening, 2013, Non-Duality Press.
© Gary Tzu 2014

ISBN: 978-1494355371

Disclaimer:

This book is designed to provide helpful information on the subjects discussed. This book is not meant to be used, nor should it be used, to diagnose or treat any medical or psychological condition. For diagnosis or treatment of any medical or psychological problem, consult your own physician or psychologist. The publisher and author are not responsible for any specific medical or psychological health needs that may require medical or psychological supervision and are not liable for any damages or negative consequences from any treatment, action, application or preparation, to any person reading or following the information in this book. References are provided for informational purposes only and do not constitute endorsement of any texts, websites or other sources.

To Marcia for sharing the beauty of the heart

To Brian and Jason for being such zestful non-dual road companions

To Craig for diving in like no brother could expect

To Catherine for her humor and this invitation

And to all the people in the groups and counseling who have joined the non-dual dance

Table of Contents

PRELUDE: *Time to Eat My Gun* vii
INTRODUCTION: *From Addiction, the Counterfeit Quest for Wholeness, to Embracing Non-dual Being* 1
The Paradox of the Journey 7

PART 1: Working Through Second Stage Recovery 10
    Chapter 1: Stalling in Second Stage Recovery 11
    Chapter 2: Honoring the Physical 20
    Chapter 3: Feeling the Pain 29
    Chapter 4: Resolving Internal Splits 40
    Chapter 5: Standing on our Two Feet with Family and Friends 51
    Chapter 6: Deconstructing Ego Identity 58
    Chapter 7: Being Authentic and Finding Meaning in the Existential Realm 62

PART 2: Hitting Bottom in Second Stage Recovery: My Separate Self Addiction 70
    Chapter 8: Discovering My Narcissism: I am the Problem 71
    Chapter 9: Seeing Hope as an Addiction: Accepting Absolute Hopelessness 78
    Chapter 10: Embracing Total Failurehood: Existence Shows Up 83

PART 3: Accelerating the Surrender Process 92
    Chapter 11: Using Almaas' Transformation of Narcissism .. 93
    Chapter 12: Letting Go of Being Saved by the Other 110
    Chapter 13: From Waiting to Direct Awareness and Inquiry 123

Part 4: Stage Three Recovery: Living with no self and dealing with re-emerging seeds of separation 129
    Chapter 14: The Mind's Fixations 130
    Chapter 15: The Unfinished Business of the Heart 140
    Chapter 16: Grasping at Survival in the Guts 146

Part 5: Abiding in Non-dual Being in Daily Life 155
    Chapter 17: The Hollow Bamboo: Letting Go of
    Personal Will 156
    Chapter 18: Touch and Let Go in Relationships 161
    Chapter 19: Enjoying Just Being 166
    Chapter 20: Accepting Failurehood and Imperfection 171
    Chapter 21: Embracing Ordinariness 179
    Chapter 22: Beyond Birth and Death, the Great
    Mystery 184
    Chapter 23: Ah *This*! 188

    References 194
    Recommended Reading 203

Prelude: Time to Eat My Gun

It was twelve years since he had first said, "My name is Randy and I am an alcoholic". Twelve years of struggle, progress, inspiration and then stalling, stalling, stalling until stalling became falling.

He looked at the gun in his lap. It was his friend, a friend who would bring him the escape, the oblivion he craved. He, or an automaton called Randy, coolly brought the gun up to his mouth. *This is it, I have nothing, no-one, I'm a worthless fraud. Time to eat my gun.*

Something broke through into automaton-Randy, his hand began to shake and the gun clattered against his teeth. The something was a feeling, a slender stab of thought, a tiny flash in the darkness. He didn't know what it was, but he found that he had put the gun down and a few seconds later the safety was on.

Ten minutes later he was on the highway to a destination twelve hours away.

He arrived suddenly at my office; I had not seen him in half a decade and I hardly recognized this old man as the vibrant, energetic Randy I used to know.

I told him to go have lunch in the downstairs cafeteria, while I shuffled my appointments and made time to be fully with him.

An hour later he was sitting in my office.

He was exhausted, at the end of the line, no energy left in him. His black, burnt out 'Dexter energy', as his wife called it (after the TV serial killer), had a draining, life-denying effect on her. There was no real intimacy, no fun, no growth in their marriage. She grew tired of trying to connect with him during evenings spent together staring blankly at the TV and she went back to her hometown without him.

After his wife left he had tried to work through the problem at home on his own, but he felt oppressed by the stifling proximity of his small town neighbors. And now here he was stuck in an ominous black energy deep in his being, a horrible hell realm that he had carried inside him for so long, but always avoided.

No-one would have guessed that he would reach this dark place. He seemed to have done everything right since that first, "I am an alcoholic". Yes, he had stopped going to meetings after a couple of years, but he had done group work, opened up to his feelings, catharted his anger, and embraced the power of the now. He had explored the works of Eastern meditation teachers and delved into mindfulness.

He had got a degree and then worked as an addictions counselor. His last post was as a wilderness addictions counselor in First Nations communities. His girlfriend moved in with him and they got married. They lived together in a northern community, where he was loved for his non-stop devotion to his job and the people.

Yet slowly over the years he grew more than tired. He was burnt out, exhausted, and the underlying black energy seemed to emerge more and more in his life. Even though he was still successful as a counselor, he was running on empty. Now his wife had gone, he was all alone in his cabin. Something was clearly wrong at the core of his being, he was immersed in blackness, an inescapable dark hell pit. He had been on a quest for recovery and wholeness, but now maybe he had to face it: his efforts had ended here, in the abyss. It all had gone wrong and the time had come for him to check out. He was at the end of the line, doomed, forsaken, and the only logical thing was to blow his brains out.

At the last moment, he had a reprieve—from where it came he could not tell—and instead of blowing his brains out he drove 700 miles. Now here he was in front of me, recounting his long tortured tale of woe, looking like an old man on the edge of a gray death. We just sat in this place together, the place of utter exhaustion and falling down.

I had no trouble being in this place with Randy, as I too had faced this hell, the moment of suicide or surrender when a person is swallowed up by the black void, the valley of the shadow of death. I knew that I had had to face it head on and that Randy, too, would need to face it before he could move on to become whole.

All the emotional work of recovery does not prepare a person for this moment. It is taking things to a different level, a depth that may have been glimpsed in the past and quickly avoided, as the whole self is now on the line.

At the time I went through this, I felt that my existence was doomed, suicide seemed like the logical answer and, like Randy, I needed to check out. Somehow, though, I knew that suicide would not resolve anything, but at the same time, I realized there was no way out or escape from this black abyss. I decided to face the terrifying darkness head on with no effort to escape, or to save myself. I simply gave up. And miraculously, the stillness of black annihilating eternity, where nothing exists, was transformed almost immediately. The beloved existence revealed itself with a brilliant all-encompassing light radiantly flashing from underneath the darkness. I knew then everything was fine.

So, as I looked over at Randy, I was relaxed and wanted to share with him both my own experience and this predicament he was in. I pointed out that he had been here before and escaped. "Now you just need to sit in this black death energy, with no judgment, and no effort to resolve it. No help is needed, and you need to stop trying to save yourself. Give it all up!" I told him.

We sat there in the silence with the ticking clock, at this end-of-the-line place with no help or hope available, and with nothing we could do, and no answer from the mind. Within minutes Randy was giggling. He found that absolutely giving up was serene and very relaxing. We just continued to sit in what some have called the valley of the shadow of death. We did not make one effort to help ourselves, we just accepted death in the moment.

Time passed quickly as we sat together. When an hour had gone by, it became apparent Randy was very relaxed—but now I needed to send him on his way. He needed to go back to his motel room so he could embrace this himself in his own aloneness. So, he bid me good day, and said he would check in with me in the morning.

The next morning, he showed up a completely different person, a radiant being, twenty years younger. I asked him how it went, and he said it was surprisingly easy. He just sat in the black energy. What we did in my office he did all alone. He did not listen to his mind trying to get him to escape. It took him only a few minutes and he was letting go and relaxing into the black energy which quickly once again had turned into vast radiant light. He did it all by himself... "Beautiful," I said to him. It was apparent all that he had needed was an invitation from me. That was enough for him to do it in his aloneness. He had gone with his perfect storm, sat in the dark valley of annihilation and death, surrendered, and the brilliant light of existence revealed itself. I said to Randy, "Welcome to abiding in non-dual being."

Introduction: From Addiction, the Counterfeit Quest for Wholeness, to Embracing Non-dual Being

This intense and at times painful craving is a deep thirst for our own wholeness, our spiritual identity, our divine source.

Christina Grof, *The Thirst for Wholeness*

We are all on the quest for wholeness—that wholeness that seems so vast, sometimes so tantalisingly close and then so unattainable. But in the Western world, we have gotten lazy, we want it fast, and we want it now. I call this the McDonald's approach to wholeness, the counterfeit path. We want it like drive-through food, we want it convenient and easy. Many of us remember the day we got hooked into that counterfeit quest for wholeness through an addictive path of one sort or another.

My twin brother was like that. He was shy, insecure, socially awkward. Once he had that first beer everything changed for him, he was in the groove, he could connect. From being an alienated outsider, in an instant he was part of the club, he was an insider. He was spontaneous, fun, the life of the party. His partying ways started in high school and really picked up while he was in university. By the time he made it to law school, while everybody was busy studying, he was holding 'Let's get sloshed' parties. Instant wholeness!

The problem is that this artificial quest for wholeness through addictive remedies can end up costing our whole lives. My brother's addictive ways did not stop at law school.

As a lawyer he combined 80-hour work weeks with late night relief drinking and binge drinking on weekends. He just wanted the release, the high, the painless remedy without doing any of the work. So when his life crumbled into a predictable midlife crisis after two decades of over-the-top legal practice work, he dived harder into alcohol, and escalated into cocaine, one night stands, and then escort services. Of course, soon he had lost his wife, his connection to his children, and then even his law practice. He went through overtly compliant trips to treatment centres in which he pretended to see the light. He used to relapse back to hardcore drinking even on the way home from the treatment centre. Then one evening, with a mixture of pharmaceuticals and booze, he went to sleep, and never woke up.

He would rather die than leave the comfort of his addiction and the pseudo relief it brought him. I miss him. He was my twin, we shared so much—and he is gone.

Myself, I never was a chronic addict in the true sense. My addiction was not to some sort of substance or process addiction, but to an underlying narcissism. I had the classic case of the American Dream; a rugged individualism through which I was going to show the whole world how very special I was. It is like that little joke: when we are born, God whispers into our ear, "You're special, you're so special" I believed it. I took it on board, hook, line and sinker. So, narcissism was my addiction. And this is why conventional second stage recovery was not enough for me, and it's likely that it's not enough for you, because as I worked on all of the pain of trauma, abandonment, disconnection, inauthenticity and emptiness, one significant insight was missing. There was a lynchpin that held it all together, and that was my fundamental narcissism, my separate self specialness. It was only when I met this narcissism head-on, and I saw how fake and shabby it was and let it all crash into the chasm of being, that I was truly able to embark on a third stage of recovery to embrace wholeness, to embrace non-dual being. This may sound strange to you, if you have been struggling with recovery from addiction, but if you have an underlying sense that there could be more, that there is another dimension to your established recovery (or your shaky recovery), then this approach can fill your unmet and almost undefined need.

Non-dual being

Non-dual being is a coming home. Not *going* home, but *coming* home. It means that we don't need to look outside ourselves for what we need when, at the same time, 'inside' we are clutching onto the sense of apartness, of isolation, grasping onto that oh-so-special 'me' with its bogus sense of entitlement. We set ourselves up to see everything as 'other' and seek to assuage our longing for completion, for wholeness, for we know not what, using substances and behaviors to soothe and reward. You will learn in these pages that there is a way to let go of addiction (and I do mean *addiction*) to our separate, special, entitled self. We can get free of the disheartening woundedness and mortality that drive us to seek outside for surcease or gratification. We will no longer feel the need to fight for survival as a separate self against all of the objects in existence that we see as 'other'.

As we let go of the grasping and identification with our separate selves, we see that our busy minds could never have saved us, and we relax into a welcoming, spacious being. Rather than escaping into the false freedom that is the prison of our addiction, we make our home in existence itself.

In this coming home, we discover that we are, and have always been, part of the mystery from which existence originates, and to our surprise we realize that there has actually been no separate self all the way along. The separate self may drop away or be seen through, but for what we lose, so much more is gained: our hearts open up into a loving intimacy with everything which is—the antithesis of addiction. Those busy minds let go of all concepts and stories to embrace a beautiful, transparent immensity and lucidity.

It was not always this way for me. When I started my journey towards non-dual being, I did not know it at the time, but I was still caught in my narcissistic stance towards existence. I was addicted to showing how special I was. When I left law to embrace transpersonal psychology and Eastern contemplative ways of being, I carried this demand of my specialness with me. Because of early successes—graduating and practicing law at 23—I thought I was a brilliant person, and the doors of life would always open up to me. I never could have predicted how wrong this was and how truly I was a misguided fool. Only as my journey towards awakening progressed, did I start to realize that I had replaced my concrete Western individualistic narcissism with the ultimate trip of narcissism, that of awakening and enlightenment—what a paradox! Even as I racked up some utterly blissful experiences, moments of ecstatic cosmic consciousness, and witnessed the vastness and eternity of existence, there was always a separate 'me' having these experiences, and so awakening escaped me. It was like the time-honored law; *wherever you go, there you are*. The 'me' was trying to get beyond the 'me'.

Only through progressive disillusionment and through using my direct awareness and inquiry, did I begin to unpack the 'me'. It was through experiencing absolute hopelessness and failurehood that the separate self was seen through. It had been quite the contradiction. I had all these lovely experiences, but at the same time I was trying to fulfill the needs of the self and survive. So, I still had to recognize that in the ultimate quest for wholeness the mind does not have the answer; I still had to work through the trauma and pain from the past in choiceless awareness, so that my heart could be loving and open; I still had to confront that central grasping and grabbing at survival in my belly. When I saw, at last, that this grasping for survival could go on forever, I was able to let go, embrace my death, and surrender to existence. Nothing to hang onto, nothing to know, nowhere to go to—and in this place, existence revealed itself.

I discovered a vast loving radiant existence that had been here all the way along—it was like a coming home to a wondrous iridescent mystery that just keeps going on and on, all revealed in this moment, 'just this'. This is one of the grand jokes of existence, that we all can go on this epic journey to find out what life is all about, and in the end it is revealed that it was all here all the way along; we just could not see it as we were too busy seeking. As we burn through the seeker, to our surprise it is revealed that the seeker is actually the sought. And here in this place of not-two, all the apparent dualities of existence merge into oneness, life and death, light and darkness, white and black, good and evil, self and other. All is experienced in the stillness of eternity in which the radiant light of existence permeates everything. This is our home, we are in an ecstatic dance of infinity, in which nothing really is ever born, and nothing dies.

It is apparent that this is what so much alcohol and drug use is about. We are trying to come home but going about it all in the wrong way. To our surprise, our home already exists within us, we just have to tune in so it can be revealed. I remember a heroin addict talking to me about how much he loved the serene, sublime, oceanic stillness he could get to with heroin, and I laughed to myself, as I knew this sublime feeling of serenity so well. It is available through just exploring our own being very deeply. In his case, the drug was only giving him a short-term chemical revelation of an aspect of himself that was already available to him, he just did not realize it. So all the alcohol and drug use can be seen as the counterfeit quest for wholeness—good intentions, desiring wholeness, but going through it using artificial, temporary means.

As we recover, I am reminded of an old Twelve Step expression, 'You don't have to ride the garbage truck all the way out to the dump.' For me, the addiction to my narcissism was so strong, so deeply rooted, that it was only when I rode my narcissism all the way to garbage dump hell that I could surrender and let go—for some of us, this seems to be our destiny. It's important to understand that letting go, losing the separate self, does not mean retreating to an ivory tower of lofty detachment from life; later on we will be looking at this over-compensatory mindset, its pitfalls and how to work through it.

This book is an invitation to you to find completion and wholeness, to work through second stage recovery fully, including a necessary descent to let go of the separate self, and to embrace third stage recovery and abide in non-dual being.

The Paradox of the Journey

With the drawing of this Love and the voice of this Calling
We shall not cease from exploration
And the end of all our exploring
Will be to arrive where we started
And know the place for the first time

T S Eliot, *The Four Quartets*

Before we start our exploration of the journey of recovery and awakening into non-dual realization, it is important to recognize the inherent paradox. The process is not a jouney from one place to another: it is really a journey from here to here.

Paradox is a word you may find often in this book. What puzzles people and seems like an inherent contradiction is that there can be an awakening, but still all the old stuff comes up and 'someone' has to let go of it. At the heart of this, is the tendency in the mind-body to believe that there is a 'somebody' to be awakened, a discrete person (and remember that the word 'person' comes from the ancient Greek word for mask). The assumption we make is that we are separate from existence, but this is not the case. We are not something different, something opposed; we are not an outsider looking in on existence. Awakening is a process of seeing that there is nobody there to be awakened and there is nothing to be awakened from. The belief in that separate self has been called hypnosis, conditioning or illusion. In any event, some of us apparent beings take a journey through time to realize eventually in this moment that there is nobody here. Later, some old habituated patterns of believing in a separate self come back, inviting a necessary re-visiting process leading to a seeing through of these patterns. There is just a seeing, with nobody here. We don't surrender. We see that there is nobody here to surrender.

Together we will explore the journey of abiding in non-dual being and no-self, but the first sticking point we reach is the obvious question: if there is no separate Gary, how can he abide anywhere? To clarify, it is more the *appearance* of Gary, this apparent mind-body, which is existence itself appearing as something that seems to be separate. For example, in daily life, when I am teaching at the university, existence passes through me in the moment, and spontaneously gives a lecture, writes a proposal or an article; it's as if the special flavor of existence that goes under the name of Gary permeates and informs each moment and there is a resting in the place of no-self awareness. So, Gary is only an appearance that seems to be abiding in non-dual being, but actually there is nobody here apart from existence itself. The appearance seems to be there and is seen to be there, but in reality there is just existence. No self is here. All of the steps of realization were actually gone through by an apparent being that took some time to realize there was nobody here all the way along.

The other side of the paradox is that, even though there was nobody here all the way along, this special flavor of existence called Gary was hypnotized to believe that it was a separate self, and so even though there was nobody here from the beginning, this apparent being had to go on a long journey of progressive steps to realize from the beginning nobody had been here all the way along. It was almost like the journey was necessary so this apparent Gary could get exhausted enough to let go of striving and grasping and slow down enough to see that in this moment there is nobody here. So, the great comedy is that I could have seen there was nobody here right from the start, but I believed something had to be done, or some effort had to be made, to attain some state, and off I went. Thankfully—after a time—I came to a place of seeing that no amount of work, effort or self-improvement would bring awakening. With seeing the futility of effort, I could just relax into the flow of existence, see nobody was here, and rest in no-self awareness. Even in this moment, nobody is here, and nothing needs to be done.

Now, as we turn to the journey of recovery and awakening, we rest in this paradox. The fullness of *what is* is always available right now, even though we may have to take some steps to realize it. What follows are some steps to help you realize that no steps are necessary, it is all already right here.

If this makes very little sense to you, but you are longing to be rid of the addiction to a substance or a behavior, or struggling with a mindset that is inconsistent with your true values, then take this as a working hypothesis, a tool that you can use and then discard. It has worked for me and for others. My dearest wish is that it will work for you too and that one day you can say with T S Eliot, 'These things have served their purpose: let them be.'

Part 1:
Working through Second Stage Recovery

Chapter 1: Stalling in Second Stage Recovery

If you haven't dealt with your underlying living problems in any focused, consistent manner, pain, pure and simple, will keep you subject to the dry-drunk syndrome.

Earnie Larsen, *Stage Two Recovery*

Ralph had been in recovery for over ten years and been in AA all of this time with not one relapse. He was sober, had a job as an addictions counselor, was in a relationship, continued to work on his communications skills and, in his own words, was a 'good guy'.

Suddenly everything collapsed around him. He was 52 and his life was a disaster. By the time he came for counseling, the wagons were already circling at work; he had had many warnings from his supervisors, who were now preparing the necessary steps to have him fired from his counseling position. He was seen as a rigid, inflexible, self-righteous, self-aggrandizing troublemaker. Furthermore, his fiancé had grown tired of his self-preoccupation and lack of empathy. She broke up with him after he would not let her father carve the turkey on Christmas Day as Ralph was 'the man of the house'.

All this came about because Ralph had never really worked on his underlying pain, depressive ways and self-righteousness. Having his world collapse around him forced Ralph into counseling, but the long delay in working on his dry drunk issues had already cost him his job and his upcoming marriage. To his surprise, Ralph had ended up getting a second descent in recovery. He had thought all of this was behind him the first time that he accepted he was powerless over his addiction.

When growth turns bad

The issue with Ralph and many others like him, is that, just because people are in recovery and abstaining from their problematic addictive behavior, whether it be alcohol, drugs, gambling or sex, their recovery can still be very much in jeopardy. Curbing the behavior in stage one recovery is only the first step. The strategies to keep from relapsing—such as going to meetings, seeing a counselor, working on triggers, cravings and stinking thinking, avoiding addict friends, not going into pubs and casinos, finding new friends and activities, and taking care of yourself—are all helpful. But has the real problem been dealt with? No, not really, as it is the underlying emotional pain underneath the addiction that is the problem as it drives the addiction. We need to ask why we have all that pain in the first place. For Ralph, it was obvious that he had not even started to look at all of the emotional pain underlying his addiction. These conclusions are borne out by the work of other pioneers in the field of addiction and my own research.

Seeing the need for a new phase in recovery from addiction, Earnie Larsen proposed a process of ongoing, or Stage Two, recovery which moves the recovering individual's attention beyond a preoccupation with abstinence to dealing with other aspects of life.[1] Larsen himself saw this second stage of recovery within the vision of AA, but there are others who doubt that AA offers what is needed to foster second-stage recovery;[2] they maintain that there are too many limiting factors in AA, such as a rigid focus on group dependence and spiritual or religious tenets and the self-fulfilling prophecy of relapse if a person leaves the Twelve

Step Fellowship. The white middle-class, patriarchal values and beliefs that dominate AA literature may also serve to limit potential.

Dr. Tina Tessina suggested that the development of autonomy is the next critical step beyond the traditional recovery process as exemplified by AA and other Twelve Step programs, and this was confirmed by a study which I carried out with a colleague.[3]

We interviewed people who were moving beyond the Twelve Steps into a second stage recovery on their own. They found themselves questioning the Twelve Step Fellowship vision of limited recovery; they needed emotional issues to be resolved; they wanted to embrace other literature, and to move forward on their own. This all culminated in people leaving Twelve Steps to embrace a further stage of recovery.[4]

Despite critiques of AA and the Twelve Steps there are many positive aspects to this approach, and it could be very limiting to throw the baby out with the bathwater in our search for autonomy and self-determination in our recovery. Larsen, for instance, argues that it is impossible to outgrow the Twelve Steps, as the spiritual wisdom contained within them is infinite. I can agree with Larsen that this applies for some people. I have met many who seem to continue to grow in the Twelve Step movement. It has been my experience, however, whether a person stays in Twelve Steps, or moves beyond them, or has been on their own path all the way along, that all paths lead eventually from the stage one focus on abstinence to the underlying emotional issues of stage two recovery. Stage two recovery is necessary no matter which path you follow—even though a person may not call it that.

Long-term recovery seems to be a dynamic process evolving over time which involves all the social and cultural, psychological and spiritual components which make up the whole person—there is no aspect of a person which can be seen in isolation.[5] As a result, recovering persons, clinicians, and researchers—all of us—are looking for a new way forward to meet the needs of a person in second stage recovery. We need a 'meta-recovery' model which supports the potential for growth in the Twelve Step Fellowship, but gives a map for those on the path to an expanded vision and new possibilities of recovery.

Second stage recovery: facing another descent

There is a logical reason for addiction. It's a skewed logic but any addiction process can be seen as a method which we use to try and climb out of the realm of negative experience into a realm of positive experience. We use the whole process of addiction to escape unresolved painful feelings such as abandonment, worthlessness and emptiness, but at the same time as we try to escape them, these negative feelings fuel our attempts at addictive self repair. It's paradoxical and it's a vicious circle, but that's what we do.

Even before our addiction became fully fledged some of us were likely to use other self-defeating behaviors such as caretaking, people-pleasing or being a martyr, to deal with our negative experiences. For true recovery we have to go deep; we have to confront and examine such behaviors which seem quite benign on the surface. They are not as harmless as they seem, but they do serve to make our reality comfortable. We use old patterns of dealing with feelings to help define what is normal for us, but this is not living authentically or living from the truth of our being; we will remain 'merely abstinent' if this is what we do. For real change, we need to examine these habits very carefully. There is good reason for this.

Unexamined and unaddressed, these habitual methods of dealing with life, addiction and recovery lead to the precarious stability of the dry drunk. This describes the compulsive drinker who has put the cork in the bottle yet continues to think alcoholically.[6] There are grandiose plans and expectations while feelings of resentment are carefully nursed by 'poor me'. The same 'poor me' will justify impulsivity, dishonesty, intolerance and a self-centeredness that masks an awful sense of inadequacy and low self-worth.[7] The problem with this precarious stability is that, with the active addiction overcome, the person has lost any perception of rock bottom, the nadir of experience which could lead to a surrender experience and true emotional sobriety.

Stalled recovery may follow the same patterns in any addiction. Patrick Carnes, the pioneer in recovery from sex, love and pornography addiction makes it clear that there is an underlying narcissism in people in active addiction and also within those in recovery; he describes this as a 'Master of the Universe' role, which we will examine in more depth later on.[8] Fuel for the addictive lifestyle is found in the deceptions, manipulations, conning, exploitation of others and attempts at escape from pain. The problem is that, when a person clears up their acting-out behaviors they are still left with all of these underlying self-centered patterns of specialness and a feeling of being beyond or above the normal rules of existence, which mask the underlying issues of inadequacy, incompleteness and not being good enough.

These qualities seem to perfectly describe the situation of Ralph, the fired counselor. Even Randy, the man with the gun to his head, in his crisis saw that his separate self was still trying to master it all.

Something is needed to take the recovering person from abstinence into authenticity, and what is called for is a second descent at the end of stage two recovery in which the whole narcissistic egoic self of the recovering person is let go of. Many of us have had meaningful surrender experiences up to this point, but only around letting go of the specific behavioral addiction or addictions. It is truly rare for people to have died to the underlying central addiction, that is their separate self. This means that it must be confronted at the end of stage two recovery so that they can make a passage into stage three recovery and abiding in non-dual being. To understand this process, we will now turn to Ken Wilber's Spectrum of Development approach and the Transformation of Narcissism approach of A.H. Almaas. Please bear in mind that, while these approaches are useful tools to take us through, I am not asking anyone to take up the entire philosophy or teachings of either Wilber or Almaas.

Wilber's Transpersonal Spectrum of Development and Three Stages of Recovery

Ken Wilber has devised a spectrum of consciousness model which incorporates conventional psychology and the contemplative traditions of both East and West.[9] He expanded this into a four quadrant model, but because we need a simple and useful map for the path to recovery, we will be looking at the original six psychological levels of Wilber's Spectrum of Development model.

1. Physical
2. Emotional self
3. Internal mind
4. Family/social
5. Ego identity
6. Existential issues

We will explore in succession second stage recovery issues for each of these developmental levels in the following six chapters.

One additional advantage of using a developmental model like Wilber's is that we can deal with the problem of disowned aspects of self, which is crucial for addicted persons in recovery.

Initially in recovery, through hitting bottom by being powerless to their addiction, a person is forced to disidentify with the addict subpersonality and begins to identify with a recovering subpersonality. This shift is dualistic in nature, with the addict subpersonality seen as all bad, and the recovering subpersonality as all good; probably this is an essential crutch or tool for some in the process of early recovery.

However, during the recovery process it is common to experience depression, boredom, irritation, listlessness or agitation, loss of vitality and spiritual or existential restlessness, which are all manifestations of frustrated growth and lack of readiness to move forward. In early recovery these symptoms may indicate the danger of possible relapse; later in recovery they may point to the frustration of blocked growth as defined by Roberto Assagioli, the pioneer in the fields of humanistic and transpersonal psychology. [10] For example, the wild risk-taking behavior of a person in the full throes of an addiction has a rebellious aspect that needs to be re-integrated later in recovery, so that a person can be authentically themselves in a healthy way and still take risks. In second stage recovery, people need to move to integrate disowned aspects of self in an often non-linear spiraling process. The process of this integration involves a shedding or reframing of beliefs that no longer serve ongoing growth and wellness; thus an overall model like Wilber's is very helpful in working through these difficult areas and coming to wholeness. Initially this wholeness will be experienced as a healthy integration, a flowering and a ripernning of the psychological self, but we come to a paradoxically greater wholeness. where we let go of the separate self and are integrated with existence itself.

Almaas' letting go of the separate self and embracing stage three recovery

The importance of letting go of the egoic separate self has long been recognized as essential in the non-dual journey to wholeness within Christianity, Buddhism, Sufism and Hinduism and by modern non-religious exponents of non-duality. This letting go is recognized by religious and spiritual frameworks, but is not dependent upon such frameworks, nor is it confined to a particular paradigm or world view. This egoic separate self can be described as a 'contraction' as it is the opposite of the expansive, welcoming wholeness that is non-dual being. Letting go of the egoic separate self usually entails some sort of overt or covert inquiry into the separate self-sense. In fact many of the modern 'teachers' see the addiction to the separate self, the ego, as the underlying addiction of the human condition.[11] The releasing of ego usually involves a process over time, going through a number of stages, but can, in some cases, be a sudden occurrence. To facilitate the movement from stage two recovery to stage three recovery we need an approach that maps out a process for working through and letting go of the narcissistic sense of a separate self.

Here we will turn to A.H. Almaas who has developed a model of growth based on the 'transformation of narcissism'.[12] This model has exciting implications for long-term recovery as it gives us the tools to work through issues typically encountered at the end of stage two recovery, such as fundamental narcissism and the inflated egoic self. Almaas' transformation of narcissism model includes such themes as discovering the empty shell and fakeness of our specialness gigs, becoming aware of the narcissistic wound, working through the great betrayal and narcissistic rage, falling into the great chasm of being, and discovering a place of loving beingness and essential identity. Almaas' model, with its focus on moving from reliance on the false egoic self to falling into beingness and essence, is pivotal in giving the recovering person the tools they need to move into stage three recovery and abiding in non-dual being.

In this book, we look at how a recovering person can revitalize a stalled recovery by looking at stage two pain issues, and then transitioning into stage three recovery.

Firstly, we utilize the first six developmental stages of Wilber's model as a map of the process of second stage recovery, to deal with all of the underlying emotional pain issues. Then we will move through the descent and hitting bottom of stage two recovery, by using Almaas' transformation of narcissism model as well as other non-dual pathways, so that a process of moving into stage three recovery can be recognized. Ultimately, it is hoped that the recovering person can transition into abiding in non-dual being, and work on issues in day to day life as a form of stage three recovery.

We will now turn our attention to Wilber's six developmental levels that explore the emotional underbelly work of second stage recovery.

Chapter 2: Honoring the Physical

You lose a sense of identity in yourself, you become running itself... I get a feeling of euphoria, almost real happiness.

Ian Thompson, marathon runner

Before we look at the first, the physical, level it is important to recognize the golden thread which runs through and holds together the entire process—wherever we are on our journey to recovery and wholeness. That thread is awareness. Awareness or the 'I am' state is one thing that we always have. We always have a sense of presence awareness. Even when we are thinking about the past or planning for the future, we are doing it from presence in this moment.

So much of the addictive pathway is a choice not to pay attention to our presence and our awareness—we would rather be anywhere but just being ourself in the moment; the journey home is always coming back to our presence and awareness—to being ourself in the present moment.

As we embrace the second stage recovery in earnest, we can recognize certain patterns. For example, addiction can be seen as a process in which the present emotional state of our experiencing is rejected for a preferred and different emotional state. In this rejection, we grasp at some remedy to change our state, whether it is having another drink, smoking a joint, trawling the internet for pornography, or placing a bet. The key here is that we are using some physical or behavioral technique to change a current emotional state to some other preferred state. So, addiction can be seen at its heart as an escape from *what is*, and the physical side of this plays a significant role.

It is also important to remember that it is not only the apparent addict who is caught in addiction and using remedies to try to change current emotional states. If we look at our lives, some of us may have, or once have had, obvious patterns of addiction such as alcohol and drugs, gambling, internet porn, smoking, video games and shopping. Yet there are so many other patterns of changing the emotional state of *what is*; they may seem a little more subtle than outright addiction, but this is not the case. How about those amongst us who work compulsively in our careers long into the night to cover up the emptiness, or the non-stop readers of self-help books feverishly looking for the answers to their problems, and even those of us who sit down at night to get lost in our favorite television series with chips and ice cream to soothe ourselves? Some of us are even waiting like hungry ghosts for our specialness to be validated by people in the world whether it be through our looks, our achievements, our possessions or even the fact that we exist. Many of us are caught up in using remedies of one sort or another to change our current state. By letting this understanding into our conscious mind, we see how addiction is a human dilemma. We all have to face it.

As we look more closely at the first level—the physical—we see that it consists of matter, sensation and perception; it is the first level that develops in life. In the first stage of recovery we spend time with interventions and techniques aimed at the physical level. In alcohol and drug addictions recovery, the physiology of the chemically addicted person is stabilized by sending the person to detox to get the drugs out of his or her system. In treatment, the person learns strategies with an emphasis on stopping the physical acting out. As a long-term smoker in recovery said, "I had to learn to not put the cigarette in my mouth." At this stage we learn not to underestimate the physical aspect of addiction, because we cannot become whole until this has been addressed.

Now to expand the physical level into second stage recovery, we can use our awareness to recognize that we have this dynamic and precious life that is our physical body. So much of the addictive lifestyle involves not taking care of our bodies, in fact destroying them. It's an extraordinary experience, when we start to use our awareness at the physical level, to find that many of our addictive patterns involve seeking out ways to make ourselves unconscious or putting our body in harm's way.

In the rituals of our addiction, we go to extremes so we are not even conscious of what is going on. Heavy drinkers find that when they drink to oblivion they can see the curtain of consciousness coming down, but they keep drinking anyway. Sex addicts describe how they are in a disassociated state in their acting out, where they lose track of what is going on even in the so-called intensity of the moment. People with intense codependent patterns may find they are in so much fear hanging on to their relationships that they are running around like scared rabbits with no awareness at all.

To curb these patterns of unawareness, I ask the people I am working with always to stay in their conscious awareness. This means just being aware of what is going on in each moment—no matter what.

In present-moment awareness we can check out how we search for oblivion, how we take this to the extreme with our addictive routine so that we may even pass out, we almost cease to exist. Now it can be seen that this is a mixing of levels in that we are craving a psychological death and rebirth, but we unconsciously play this out physically. So, rather than all these mini unconscious physical deaths of passing out to oblivion, maybe we need to take this need to escape or blot out our psychological suffering and bring it into our conscious awareness.

With cravings, too, we can see the whole process of trying to escape to a 'better' place. Check it out if you have not done so in your recovery. See that what arises is an uncomfortable feeling or symptom in the body. See how you reject this arising as unbearable or unmanageable, and a craving arises for some method to get you out of this state. The craving is the promise of a more pleasant future. Notice, though, that the craving is just a temporary arising—it is finite, it will pass. Rather than acting on the craving, let the craving just be in awareness and see how it dissolves by itself. Do nothing. By not grabbing it, you are circumventing the addictive process. The craving dissolves by itself. You are left to deal with the original uncomfortable state. In the next chapter, we will go more deeply into working with uncomfortable emotional states. For now, it can be safely summarized as 'what you avoid, persists'. This points towards the benefit of sitting with our emotions—just sitting with them and being conscious of them in the present moment.

Follow your bliss

Beyond the more obvious physical aspects of abstinence and awareness of cravings, many initiatives can be undertaken at this level including attention to diet, vitamins and working out—whether that be weight training, long distance running, yoga, martial arts, biking or swimming or some other activity. As William Glasser, the founder of Reality Therapy, emphasized, all of us benefit from developing positive habits of wholeness maintenance.[1] Like most Western psychologists, Glasser is seeing wholeness as the integrated body-mind. Later, we will see the importance of non-separation in wholeness. It is clear that the neurochemistry of the recovering person can be naturally enhanced, replacing the previous habits of self-medication with activities that naturally enhance healthy, balanced neurotransmitter functioning.[2]

I always ask a person with whom I am working with two questions: *Does all of your body feel alive with energy? Do you have a sense of energy flowing through your body?* This is just a quick way to see if a person's body has opened up so the flow of existence is passing through. Body can be used to move beyond body. For me, it is just a quick way to see if the body has become like a temple and open to dimensions of consciousness and energy.

If you have answered no to these two questions, that is okay. You just have to find a way to open up the body naturally. The way I like to look at this is to use Joseph Campbell's expression to "follow your bliss".[3] Find a physical activity that you really enjoy, and keep up with that. The reason that I like to use the bliss model is that, if you have ever been an addict for a while, you already know how personal will failed you. It was there for a while, and then tiredness, hurt, loneliness or exhaustion came, and it went away. Picking yourself up by the bootstraps of personal effort doesn't last for long. Instead, find something you love to do to keep you tuned in at the physical level, and go with that. Find and follow your bliss.

In my own case, I found that, when I really started my second stage recovery in earnest, I was not in touch with my body at a physical level. I had read some articles about the runner's high but did not really believe in such a thing. I started running a half hour a day. At first, I did not notice much of a change. But, after I got use to my running I noticed a funny thing: after the first five minutes, my body would just take over naturally, and run effortlessly. As well, I noticed that some days while running I could feel myself in the spontaneous flow of existence. Over time, as my runs increased to daily runs of an hour, it seemed I could run effortlessly, and sometimes I would fall into not only a runner's high, but a cosmic high. I seemed to be at one with nature and the cosmos around me. The body at times seemed to just be able to run by itself, with no effort at all. For me, I noticed the trick was to run in nature as much as possible. To get connected.

And about fifteen years ago, I found out it is better if I run every day for an hour. It is just easier that way. This way the mind does not have to make any decisions. I do not listen to "I am too tired", "I am too busy", "I am feeling lousy", that sort of thing. I will not run only on days when I am really unwell or injured. People are amazed when they find out I run every day. In reality it is not harder—it is actually easier that way.

If I feel that the energy in my body is blocked, I consciously set up some intense hill running. This is easy to do as there is a huge hill at the end of my normal coulee run along a river. Instead of slowing down for this rather long steep hill, I speed up. I run up the hill as fast as I can, and keep going, even if out of breath. It clears the energy blocks in the body very fast. I have described this to friends as being like taking a refreshing dip in a cool lake on a hot day.

What I have described here is what works for me, but the key for all of us is to find some habit to keep setting the body free. It is not hard as we are not trying to compete or win medals. Just find some way in which you can get into the physical body and enjoy... Keep up with that. Follow your bliss and turn every cell of your body alive with energy.

Intervening with our bodies

I like the way William Glasser described how, before he saw his depressed clients for a psychotherapy session, he would have them go out for a run. Many of these clients' problems went away just by running before their session. When I talk to my addictions counseling classes, we laugh at how we all can think we have such huge problems, and then we go for a physical workout for an hour, and most of our problems are gone. I am not saying, though, that you can use the physical body to deal with all your issues. I love running, and will occasionally go for two-hour daily runs on holidays, as it is so exhilarating, but I know I can't keep it up in daily life. I always return to the one-hour runs. Taking things to the extreme the other way, with obsessive training sessions, is not conducive to progress in recovery. The important thing is just finding a way to keep tuned with the physical, and embracing the middle path.

Sometimes issues that present as clinical problems are caused by people not paying attention to the physical. Let me give an example from my clinical practice. As a university counseling professor, I work with many practicing counselors in my own clinical practice. Typically, they are well experienced in their field, have heard of this non-dual transpersonal work and want to be challenged.

Lynn was a counselor in the field who consulted with me over her concern that after many years of being on a healing journey of recovery, she was now in a period of low energy and low-grade depression. Before exploring the emotional reasons behind her current state, we looked at what was going on now in her life that was different from before, and we found out she had stopped physically working out six months ago. She no longer had a space in her life in which she could physically clear out her energy; this was something particularly significant for her because of the vicarious trauma she was picking up working as a counselor. She had a problem which affects many therapists—working all day with clients who told tragic heartbreaking stories of sexual abuse got to her at the physical level, as well as the emotional. We will see that in the next chapter so much of energy work is to let things flow. To get her flow back, I encouraged her to re-start her long distance running plan immediately. Two weeks later, she reported feeling much better, having energy at her disposal, and feeling herself again. She still had some intense emotional work to do, but at least now the energy was flowing through her body.

Not all issues of stalled recovery can be easily resolved through a physical remedy. It nevertheless is very helpful to keep working at the physical level to keep the body opened up and attuned.

Below, I have included some awareness exercises to try out. If these exercises do not appeal to you, then simply proceed to the next chapter, once you have read them through.

Exercise 1: **Embracing body awareness**

✻

Firstly, let us work in the moment on our awareness of cravings.

> Notice an uncomfortable feeling or symptom arising in the body:
>
> *See how you reject this arising as unbearable or unmanageable*
>
> Notice how a craving arises in your body-mind
>
> *See how this is a method to get you out of this state*
>
> *See how the craving is the promise of a more pleasant future*
>
> Rather than acting on the craving, do nothing
>
> *See how by not grabbing it, you are circumventing the addictive process*

Notice how the craving eventually dissolves by itself

See that you are left to deal with the original uncomfortable state

Now, again do nothing to change it

See how the state eventually changes and eventually dissolves by itself

All just in awareness

We want to enjoy our bodies and physical movement. Choose a physical activity that you really enjoy.

Enjoy a physical activity for 30 minutes:

See how, rather than just trying to get it over with, you can enjoy each moment

Stay in present-moment awareness

See how by just enjoying each moment of the activity, it can be fun and relaxing

Keep your mind out of it, and just enjoy the physicality

See how easy it is to do when you are enjoying yourself

Commit to a regular time to do your activity that works for your schedule and energy

See how it is much easier when rather than using will power you enjoy the activity

You are following your bliss

Chapter 3: Feeling the Pain

To let it go, you have to let it flow. You can't fully let go of a dark emotion until you've experienced its truth.

Miriam Greenspan, *Healing Through the Dark Emotions*

It was a weekend Gestalt workshop I attended just after starting a master's degree in counseling. A woman there, in her early twenties, seemed very quiet and shut down. The facilitator started working with her on Saturday morning, and even though she said nothing about her anger, soon had her 'beating the mats'. What happened next was amazing: the woman was *trying* to be angry, but all of a sudden her body took over. A fury went through her, and for about ten minutes, she pounded the mats with rage and intensity in a frenetic release of what had been held in for so long. When she had finished, the group asked her how she was doing, and she replied, "Much better!" We did not even need to know the answer as she was glowing with energy. It was like she was flowing again and had accessed her own resources, all by going with her pain and acting out her anger.

This idea that the energy needs to flow has been a big part of my own healing work and my work with clients since then. Not only have I committed to a daily one-hour run for years, but I have even taken it a step further. I realized at a deep self-other level there was a lot of primal pain there, so I catharted out my pain through intense yelling and primal screaming. If it was really bad, I would go out into the woods and yell at trees. I have made a few minutes of oral catharsis followed by a quiet meditation part of the opening exercises we do in the non-dual groups that I have facilitated over the last number of years. It helps people regain their flow if lost in life. For me, Greenspan's words ring true: "To let it go, you have to let it flow."[1]

Where does all of this pain come from? When we are young, we began to develop emotional boundaries through the development of a separated-individuated self. There is the self and the other—the other with whom we start to develop an emotional connection. People with severe addiction issues often regress back to this stage as their world contracts and is reduced to the connection with their addiction. After a prolonged addiction, it can become just the person and the bottle (or the porn, or whatever we use). In stage one recovery there can be some movement in replacing the reliance on the 'other' of the addiction ritual, but if we are working towards wholeness and fundamental freedom from addiction, then we can go deeper and further. It is common for the person who has regressed into chronic addictions issues and then committed themselves to recovery to be marking time instead of going forward and growing.

This means there are some difficult issues to face in stage two recovery. People in recovery can be immobilized in self-other pain and emotional wounds which they had previously covered up through their substance use. It is essential to work on this fundamental self-other stance and try to reclaim a trust in life.

The addictions process is how we try to replace negative experiences with positive experiences, according to Firman and Gila,[2] and I think most of those touched by addiction would agree. It's often the haunting unresolved negative feelings of being unlovable, inadequate, and worthless that we are trying to escape. These negative feelings which we are trying to avoid lie underneath our attempts at healing, rather like a wound that has healed on the surface only. The tragic impact of neglect and abuse can magnify this negative dynamic. If we look at the central feelings of these experiences we can see how much hidden pain, shame, abandonment and emptiness drive the addictive cycle.

The key here in second stage recovery is to go purposefully to that unwanted place—the place we used to try and avoid by self-medication. To find the wholeness we are seeking we need go to this place of dark pain and embrace acceptance of pain rather than escape. Otherwise we will remain divided and conflicted within. This seems counterintuitive at first because we have been conditioned to think that our pain is unbearable and we have learned to never look directly into the face of our pain. To our surprise we can find that, by being one with our pain through adopting a no-judgment stance, the sting of the pain dissolves and we discover a healing essence within it. The transformation of our pain into healing essence means that we no longer have to escape from it through some addictive process; nor do we have to be attached to it, as we merely sit in the pain itself and reclaim the energy.[3]

In my own life, I have reconnected with this underlying pain, and learned to accept the feelings of inadequacy, emptiness, abandonment and being unappreciated, and just let the energy flow. When I first started opening up to this pain, I found turbulent rivers of anger, sadness and hatred and, soon after that, loneliness, emptiness and betrayal. It was a shock for me to discover how all of these deep dark feelings could be just sat in, and the pain could be transformed. I remember early on discovering the powerful paradoxical nature of loneliness. When I sat in loneliness without trying to change it, it transformed all by itself into a beautiful spacious aloneness. Even more shocking was when I sat in hatred, and accepted hatred, it transformed itself into a vast, dark, loving spaciousness that could easily set boundaries.

Over the years, however, I also discovered that there can be some crystallized thought-forms attached to these deep emotions that have to be looked at. Stephen Wolinsky describes how we need to become aware of false core drivers and false compensatory systems that have been at play in our deep emotions for the greater part of our life.[4] It can be quite an eye opener to realize that we have been driven our whole life by a core belief which we have mostly kept out of our awareness. Here, by sitting in our worst experiences and feelings, and simply by asking what is the worst part about this experience, we can discover a core belief that we have inadvertently taken on and made central to our psychological system. Common examples of these statements are: "I am worthless", "I am bad", "I am out of control", "I am unlovable", and "I am deficient" and even such intense statements such as "I shouldn't have been born".

We lose our awareness of these core beliefs through what Wolinsky called our "false self compensator" which attempts to heal, transform, psychologically fix or use a spiritualized remedy in an attempt to overcome the false core. Tragically, our attempts to overcome the false core through our defensive systems only reinforce that false core, because at a deep level we believe and accept its premise that we are somehow deficient in ourselves. Instead, we can help long-held core beliefs melt away simply by allowing ourselves to become aware of these core statements, and letting them dissolve by being mindful and present. The key here is that we have to sit in, and with, our false core directly and allow it to dissolve through non-judgmental awareness. Myself, I was shocked to discover a false and painful core driver that "I am insignificant". Rather than using a false self compensator of trying to show how significant I was—which cannot work as it is based on a shaky foundation—healing easily happened by just staying in the preverbal 'I am'. Staying in mindful presence, the statement dissolved by itself and the accompanying energy transformed from an inner dark pit of insignificance to a vast loving full spaciousness.

Sometimes people have dark emotions and false core beliefs, for which they have suffered terrible consequences, and from which they still want to run away. Tony had spent hard time in jail for his addictive behavior, and for beating up a fellow guest at a house party when he was drunk. He had learned to put on the persona of a tough guy. But now he had been out of jail for years, and even worked as a counselor after going to college for his degree. He had come to work with me in counseling, as he could feel there was something dead inside himself. It was as if he was frozen inside, numb. When I asked him to express his frozenness he could not go there, it would be too hard, he claimed. He might get out of control, and the last time he did that he beat somebody up. So, I said to him, "Why don't you talk to this empty chair as if it is life itself? Tell life how you feel." He kind of shrugged his shoulders, but went along with my suggestion. He started off by saying, "I am angry at you for letting me down." "Louder!" I said to him. "Screw you!" he yelled at the empty chair. I gave him a tennis racquet and he started pounding on the couch. "Fuck you! Fuck you!" He yelled at the top of his lungs and smashed the tennis racquet in a frenzy of release. After a few minutes, I asked him how he was doing. "Great," he said, "I feel alive."

I asked Tony if he felt in his belly, what type of thoughts were coming up. He said something very interesting: "I am out of control." No wonder he did not want to give himself over to the energy: there were painful consequences on the last occasion and he went to jail. But instead, I just invited him to stay in this out of control place with no judgment. Up came the thought: *I am unlovable.* Here, he just stayed with his belly awareness, and made no attempt to change his feelings of being out of control or being unlovable. He quickly found an amazing thing: there was just *spaciousness* in his belly. He was okay with being out of control; in fact the spaciousness was just a natural factor of his existence. And even his unlovableness had transformed into a welcoming, loving spaciousness. He reported he had not felt this good in years.

So, the key here is to see how we run away from our dark emotions, and the accompanying false core drivers; we believe they would be too painful to handle. One emotion we particularly do not want to touch is hatred for other people, which is often buried deeply within us.

Crystal attended one of my weekend therapy groups to work on an issue of the looming dark feelings she had towards her graduate school classmates. The therapy group was not getting much energy from her; they could not sense an authentic voice in her, so directly and indirectly they called her a manipulative liar. When asked what her response to this was, Crystal said she was "fine". "Really?" I asked. "Yes," she said, "I am fine." I asked her how she was feeling in the body right now, and she said, "Numb." I asked her instead of shutting down what did she want really to say to the group. She asked me, "What do you mean?" I said to her, "Aren't you mad at them for accusing you of being a manipulative liar, and wouldn't you like to tell us all off?" She smiled. I said to her, "Go for it!" She got up and looked around the room and meekly said, "Fuck you." "Come on!" I urged, "Say it like you mean it." She raised her voice, and said, "Fuck you!" The group laughed as they still did not believe a word she said. Finally, she shouted it at the top of her voice. The piercing shrill voice from deep within the center of her being filled the room up with intensity. Everybody smiled, and said, "Thank you for that." She had burst out of her frozen shut-down state into a dynamic intensity. I asked how she was feeling now. She said, "Ecstatic… I am giddy." It was as if the icy place inside her had thawed and melted: now she was flowing. She said, "I feel like myself again, and I can relate to my classmates and deal with what comes up in the group."

At this level, we are looking at opening up our emotional relationship to the world in the moment, no matter what that is. This is the time to stop avoiding the dark emotions—hatred, anger, grief, sadness, despair and abandonment.

Abandonment is a tricky and complex issue; we can be carrying around a fear of abandonment for decades. We keep trying to make a close connection with others, but there seems to be something missing, something deficient, because of the black hole inside us.

Holly was like that. In her mid twenties, in recovery for co-dependency which went hand in hand with substance abuse and sexual addiction, for years she had been running tapes of perfectionism, idealized body image and co-dependency. The one place she did not want to visit, let alone admit and explore, was the deep sense of abandonment which she had carried since finding out she was left by her birth mother to be adopted. She had been feeling unlovable and abandoned since she was an eight-year-old child. Now, almost twenty years later, I invited her to sit with and in her feeling of abandonment, and the sense of "I am unlovable". This was something she had avoided as long as she could remember, fearing that this would be too painful to process. She was invited to go to this awful place which she had avoided for so long, to breathe and to stay in the present. Initially, a feeling of panic came over her as the pain of abandonment felt too intense for her to handle, but I reminded her to stay mindful, without judgement. Suddenly, the experience began to transform itself as she started to feel the abandonment as a vast aloneness energy in the moment. Soon she discovered, to her amazement, that she felt peaceful and spacious in that place of abandonment which had once terrified her. Over the next few weeks, this shift at her core level resulted in a similar shift in her everyday life; for the first time she was relaxed in her aloneness, and did not desperately need to cling to the validation of others. A deep emotional pain was healed.

Betrayed by life

Sometimes, even when a person has been in recovery for years, this basic stance of self-other pain has not been addressed. Maury was referred to me for therapy by a local addictions centre. He was a 42-year-old recovering drug addict. Having lived the life of a drug addict and a male prostitute for many years, he began his path of recovery four years ago by going to a halfway house and attending AA and NA meetings. For the last three years he had worked as a teacher's aide. Maury felt that he was now at a stage of barely hanging on and feared that he was about to fall back into an addictive path of self-destruction.

Maury had been to many social workers and counselors in the past but came to me because he heard that my approach might be able to offer something different. I told him that, as a developmentally oriented, transpersonal, non-dual therapist, I would not focus dogmatically on one technique but I could offer instead a variety of techniques and approaches, which were most suited to his situation and his needs. These interventions could help him work through the wounds and the pain underlying his addiction, so that he could come to a place of healing and be able to enjoy his present life, including both aloneness and intimacy in relationships. As Maury's abstinence from drugs was well into its fourth year, we decided to start our work together on the emotional pain underlying his addiction.

Maury had already hit rock bottom four years ago and had been confronted with his chronic addiction and chaotic lifestyle. He had surrendered to his powerlessness over his drug use, entered into a treatment program and attended outpatient counseling. He had seen how much his life had become preoccupied with cocaine. Going to Twelve Step meetings helped him realize that he could not afford a relapse, as he would resume his drug use where he last left off. He was also well aware of the personal litany of lies, cheating and deception that had been a constant part of his cocaine lifestyle. But now, four years into recovery, he could see his life was on hold; he was, in his view, in a rut. At the heart of his concern was the fact that his pain and misery were still there and seemed to be destroying a precious intimate relationship with his girlfriend. He had to deal with the issues of pain and low self-esteem underlying the addiction—the issues that still remained, even though he was no longer using.

This was a second visit to Wilber's second level of development. At his first visit Maury recognised that he had descended into being a completely self-preoccupied drug user with his cocaine addiction. This was an absolutely crucial insight at the time that gave him the impetus to eschew his addictive lifestyle. Now, Maury was seeing that the issue was more complex and that he needed to deal with his basic self-other orientation to life. He had to deal with the pain underlying his addiction that kept him entrenched in the wound of the self.

To begin the process, I invited Maury to share his emotional pain out in the open where healing could take place. To do this, we had to re-visit the sources of his pain, starting with a childhood of physical abuse and abandonment by his family, foster home placements, and the terrible lifestyle of living on the street at a young age. We continued the process by looking at the ongoing pain in his adulthood and how he tried to anesthetize that pain through drugs, even though the drugs only added to his pain in the longer term. Maury shared his many unsuccessful attempts to get off the street and start a new life and all the times he had found himself returning to the back alleys of the drug world. As we processed his pain, Maury was relieved just to talk about it and get it all out in the open. He had learned the lesson of fundamental mistrust early in his life, which had shaped his self-other relationships. The less holding and nurturing available in the environment, the more a person will develop unhealthy mechanisms for dealing with an environment that is not trustworthy. For a long time, cocaine was the only thing Maury could count on, and he had lived the life of the isolated self. Now he needed to process his feelings of betrayal.

I asked Maury to face an empty chair and express all the feelings of betrayal, resentment and "the dirty rotten deal" he had gotten from life. He really got into it, and let out his long-held dark pain with a vengeance. I then suggested that he should sit in the pain, and scream as loud and desperately as he could. I urged him to let all the pain out. He sobbed broken-heartedly as he expressed his pain for the first time. After the session, he reported feeling exhausted but having more energy. This was a powerful turning point in our work together. Maury had learned to befriend his pain.

We can see how the key at this stage is to embrace these deep emotions and the accompanying pain, without running away from them. When we let the painful energy flow, emotions start thawing and transforming themselves. We see, too, how we can bring the accompanying false core beliefs into our awareness and then let them dissolve through our awareness—rather than trying to fix them. I suggest that you try the *Sitting in our Pain* exercise on the following page.

In the next chapter, we will look at how to go even deeper into the healing process by resolving psychological splits.

Exercise 2: Sitting in our pain

✵

The key here is to go the unwanted place which we used to self-medicate ourselves out of. Now we need to go to that dark pain and embrace acceptance of pain rather than trying to escape it.

> Practice sitting in your pain for thirty minutes a day without trying to fix or escape it:
>
> *See how trying to escape it or manage the pain, intensifies it*
>
> Notice any judgments or critical statements and do nothing about them
>
> *See how these judgments dissolve by themselves as as you realize they are just thoughts*
>
> Remain in your present-moment awareness with your pain
>
> *See how the pain loosens, transforms and dissolves by itself, all through doing nothing*
>
> *Pain is transformed by being one with it*

Chapter 4: Resolving Our Internal Splits

The pain that you create now is always some form of non-acceptance, some form of unconscious resistance to what is.

Eckhard Tolle, *The Power of Now*

I can remember the day I discovered something unique about fear and anxiety. Fear and anxiety would come up in relation to something significant that was arising in the next day or two; a media interview, for instance. I used to feel the fear ahead of time, and try to manage it with some type of remedy, a technique which seemed to only increase the fear. So, instead of that approach, I switched to doing nothing. I did not try to manage the fear at all. This meant dropping all of the fear management strategies as well as the critical voice which was saying: *Oh my God, look at how fearful you are.* I just dropped listening to all the voices and thoughts, and returned to the intensity of this moment. Paradoxically, and to my amazement, by doing nothing to change it, the fear dropped by itself, and just turned to intense energy. By giving up the struggle, my wholeness was reclaimed. It seemed like I was no longer fighting with myself, using different parts of my psyche. Instead, I was using the whole mind.

Here we are talking about the third developmental level, the internal mind, representing the development of the intra-psychic representational self; this is where we tend to get caught in intra-psychic splits. In Freudian psychology, this is described as the development of the id, ego and superego and the resulting intra-psychic conflicts between these parts. These conflicts manifest as inhibition, anxiety, obsession, guilt and depression. Our id is the biological pleasure and avoidance of pain principle—so familiar to people with addictions issues. The superego is the judging moral conscience, arbiter of right and wrong. The ego is the manager which tries to work this all out.

At this level, substance abuse is seen as a false path, an attempt to resolve intra-psychic conflicts by chemical soothing of anxieties and fears; it will not lead to wholeness—neither the wholeness of an integrated and healthy psyche nor the wholeness that is the non-separation from life itself. This applies, too, to behaviors that work on the pleasure/reward systems of our own neurochemistry. As we work on this level, it becomes clear that we may have unconsciously set up psychic splits to deal with trauma experiences. Ironically, it is usually the case that it is not the experience itself that keeps us frozen, but our own judgmental, split-off critical voice that says: *This is terrible!* It leads to dissociative avoidance of the experience altogether. In recovery we are looking to resolve the intra-psychic conflict through re-integration of repressed, disconnected or alienated aspects of being, or through restoring balance where other split-offs have been overemphasized and over-used to compensate for imbalances.

So, at this internal level, we can recover and reclaim wholeness, by resolving the psychological splits that have resulted in us disowning aspects of our self. In the first stage of recovery, our inner resources are used to bring the id under control. Here we avoid pubs, liquor stores and old friends from our life of addiction, and focus on ensuring that we have stopped having that next beer, the next line of cocaine, or placing the next bet. But as we put our id in check, as we curb our behaviors, we have to deal with the whole issue of the critical voice which typically may have under-functioned in the chronic phases of our addiction. Now in recovery, its self-loathing nature can mushroom, and we can be overwhelmed with self-criticism.

So, in the second phase of recovery, the first place to look for splits is in that critical inner voice. A great deal of our own inner resources and energy can be dammed up, frozen or held back from use in day to day life—all because of that inner criticism—and we may feel that we are not operating at our full potential.

Firstly, to help clarify the situation, we can put our critical voice in an empty chair, and then move over and, temporarily, take on its role by expressing a typical derogatory dialogue to the waiting self. Then, when we move back to our original seat, it can be quite liberating to defeat the critical voice, to tell it to "leave me alone" or whatever it takes to dismantle the voice. This process goes further than cognitive therapy, which tries to rationally debunk the critical voice.[1] Here, we can experience an energetic, deeply felt, emotional catharsis and healing in defeating the voice, and feel a sense of freedom from its carping, belittling and cramping comments.

This process of debunking the critical voice can be taken a step further, when it is realized that we have introjected the critical voice of another internally. A person can have carried a parent's or spouse's voice inside for many years. We can externalize the voice by role-playing the person who criticizes or belittles us. Then we switch back to being ourselves and set boundaries with the person and that critical voice which we have internalized. No longer will we allow that voice to limit us and hold us back from our potential—we are free to experience life without the entrenched critical voice within. All of this can be done alone or with a counselor.

To reclaim assertion energy, there is an exercise which can be used to help the recovering person to use the energy that has been stored up as repressed anger. This anger energy that is tied up and hidden from conscious awareness becomes what Jungians would call the shadow.[2] The shadow of repressed so-called dark energy can serve as a vital reservoir that needs to be released so that the energy can be re-integrated into conscious awareness.

For example, Wendy, a young woman in her early twenties, had been in recovery for five years after a turbulent adolescence. All this time she had been begging for acceptance from her corporate executive father. For many years she withheld her authentic voice from him, and now in a role play, I encouraged her to embrace her shadow self, and express her anger to her imaginary dad who was sitting in the empty chair. The emotional catharsis that follows was intensified when Wendy raised her voice and expressed loudly to her dad, "I am angry at you, dad. It's over, I can't beg for your acceptance anymore." Soon Wendy became more confident in setting boundaries and claiming her freedom and shouted, "Screw you, dad, I have to live my own life!" The session over, Wendy was shocked at how energized and exuberant she felt. She was reacquainted with how much energy she had at her disposal, and her ability to set boundaries.[3] She was becoming whole again.

Abuse and trauma

For a person in recovery, there may be a very long-term pattern of judging and splitting from the world, which was already in play when the addiction started. Myself, I had to go back and deal with childhood trauma. I remember working on this as I was dealing with the emotional pain issues of second stage recovery. Under the guidance of a counselor, I accepted the suggestion to lie down on a mat and unlock my repressed energy. I pounded the mat furiously, screaming, "I hate you, I hate you!" at my imaginary dad. The session escalated and suddenly I was expressing an energy that I never knew I had within; I let out a deep gut-wrenching primal scream and I was done—released, and with so much energy at my disposal.

The problem was, though, that after a few weeks I wanted to do it again. My counselor told me, "Gary, this seems to be getting to be old hat for you." I wanted to disagree, but knew the comment rang true. I was getting used to catharsis. I enjoyed the release of energy, but the whole routine was becoming predictable. There seemed to be a missing piece to the puzzle, and it took me a few years to figure it out. Catharsis is not enough: what is needed is insight and a new way of being, so that trauma does not recur, and old trauma can be healed.

Healing through choiceless awareness

As an emerging transpersonal psychologist, I had already read extensively about the seeker's dilemma. I started making some connections between this predicament and the pain of trauma, which opened up the possibility of new ways of being with trauma. The words of Sosan, the third patriarch of Zen, pointed to a new way:

> *The Supreme Way is not difficult; it just precludes picking and choosing... To see the Way with your own eyes, quit agreeing and disagreeing. The battle of likes and dislikes—that's the disease of the mind.* [4]

It now seemed that the painful aspect of my trauma was my stance against the experience. It was not the actual experience that was the painful problem, but my stance that "this is terrible". This stance creates the split in my mind. In a similar vein, J. Krishnamurti continually warned that the ideal of *what ought to be* needs to be dropped to focus on what *is*.[5]

Seeing that I needed to drop the judging, comparing voice was a tremendous realization for me. I could now see how this critical voice of judgment was keeping me locked into the trauma. This realization is similar to the emphasis in transpersonal psychology on dropping the separate-self stance in the movement towards wholeness. The complaining 'me' voice could be dropped. This is a letting go of the split mind. There can be experiencing without the complaining experiencer.

With this new awareness, I re-explored the significant traumas I had gone through in my life, the physical abuse from my dad, the brain cancer death of my mother, and being fired on two occasions. I was shocked to find that, if I just watched these experiences with no judgment, no critical self comment, something shifted. I could watch these experiences and for the first time re-experience them without a deep conflict. I did not have to hang onto these experiences by telling myself how horrible they were. I could let go.

Thus, choiceless awareness of trauma and re-integrating energy became a vital healing theme for me and for my work with clients. For example, I was working with Scott, who had been in recovery for about two years from a drug addiction. He was shocked to realize that his ongoing moment-to-moment thinking involved an automatic judgmental voice that constantly criticized and gave a negative perspective on everything. The tough part of this was that most of the criticism was directed at Scott. He was constantly telling himself how much of a loser he was, or what a dirty rotten deal he kept getting from life. I could see that much of his energy was still caught at level three of Wilber's model, the state of being intra-psychically split. Part of him was experiencing life, and part of him was constantly judging how terrible things were.

It was an eye-opener for him to realize how much of his time he spent in this negativity and how the critical inner voice was constantly rejecting present moment experience.

To help unlock this pattern, we revisited Scott's past. The theme of betrayal had started early in his life when he had chosen to move out of his childhood home as a teenager to escape a tyrannical father. This moving out, it turned out, was a transition from the frying pan into the fire, as one tough living situation followed another in the downbound train of addiction. As a young person, his superego had concluded: *This is very bad, I must be a very bad person to have this happen to me.* He continued the same type of self-talk through into his adult life. It was evident that Scott was wounded in his ego development and had a feeling of toxic shame deep inside him. He had internalized his hard knocks as if there was something wrong with him—wrong at the very core of his being.

After a few intense sessions, during which Scott catharted his pain, I began to feel we were moving fast, but going nowhere, while Scott reported that he was growing tired of all of this expressing pain work. Thus I invited him to try something different. "Witness all you have gone through in your life without judgment", was my instruction. To help Scott, together we went through the day his father threw him down the stairs, and Scott decided to leave home. Scott had always avoided the pain around this experience, so now was his opportunity to sit in that pain without judgment. I suggested he imagine that he had just been thrown down the stairs by his father and be in that place, without inner comment. I asked him to let go of that critical voice, the voice which passed judgment on how awful his situation was, and just sit in the pain of abandonment, hurt and betrayal—just be with it. As we sat there for a few minutes, suddenly Scott replied, " I feel very sad, but it is okay. All of this pain and hurt is just turning to a loving broken-heartedness, an appreciation of life." Without judgment, all the dark emotions in Scott miraculously transformed themselves into a loving spacious essence.

Scott was excited to go home and try this no judgment approach to his whole life. He returned the following week bubbling with excitement. While doing this exercise, he had the sudden realization that he did not have to hang onto his past anymore. He could just *be*. He did not have to hang onto this feeling of betrayal, unjustness and victimhood. He stated proudly, "I can let go of the garbage." He also saw how he could use this new insight in present day life, in that he could stop judging present day experiences as being negative and learn to participate more freely in the moment.

Discovering the limits of catharsis

It is clear that, although catharsis at an emotional and physical level can be very helpful, an important insight is to see the role of the critical self and drop that judgment through simply learning to have no judgment about the experience. Then we are free to feel the experience and the emotional energy that is involved without judgment. This leads a person to reclaim all energy and essence, an intense healing in itself. Check this out for yourself by trying the awareness exercises on the following pages. As this healing takes place, though, we need to learn to stand on our own two feet with family and friends, and in the next chapter we will deal with the family-social level.

Exercise 3: **Dismantling the critic to reclaim your energy**

※

Due to inner criticism, a great deal of our own inner resources and energy can be dammed up or frozen, or repressed from day to day life. We need to reclaim that energy.

> Choose a situation or issue in which the inner critic pops up:
>
> *Try to choose a situation in which the critic has gotten nasty*
>
> Sit in one chair with an empty chair facing across from you
>
> *Remember all of the nasty things the critic has said to you*
>
> Now go sit in the empty chair and face your original seat
>
> Play the role of the critic and with your voice express all its criticisms
>
> *See if you can enjoy saying all these criticisms out loud*
>
> Now go back to your original seat, and be yourself.
>
> With all of your energy, debunk the critic sitting across from you with fierce intensity
>
> Yell "Leave me alone" or "Shut up" or whatever it takes to dismantle the voice
>
> *See how freeing it is to smash and defeat the inner critic*
>
> Notice afterwards how much more energy you have at your disposal

Secondly, debunking the critical voice process can even be taken a step further, when it is realized that one has introjected the critical voice of another person internally.

> *You can role play the person from whom the critical voice has come:*
>
> Go to the other chair and be that other person, and face yourself
>
> *Get in touch with all those criticisms that you carry around with you*
>
> As the other person, talk to the original chair as if you were sitting in it
>
> *Enjoy sharing all the nasty judgments and criticisms by being that other person*
>
> When done, return to the chair of your original self
>
> *See that you are fed up and realize enough is enough*
>
> Let the other person have it full throttle, release yourself, be as nasty as it takes
>
> *See how wonderful it is to reclaim your energy and be assertive*
>
> Make sure you have verbally cut the cord of enmeshment
>
> *See how much more energy you have at your disposal*
>
> Enjoy your freedom

Finally, practice saying all the dark shadowy things that you have wanted to say to somebody but never had the courage to say.

Imagine the person sitting in an empty chair across from you:

Let them have it with all your anger, hurt, and rage

See how you can really enjoy expressing all your pain

Take it to the max, and let go of control

See how you are accessing pools of energy that have been dormant

Really give it to the person for all of the pain you have felt over the years

Repeat key phrases, and raise your voice, and let yourself totally go for it

See how at some point you become tired

When exhausted, stop

Notice how you have much more energy than when you started

See how even though you expressed your rage, your energy now feels more loving

By expressing your dark emotions, you are freer, more open and flowing

Chapter 5: Learning to Stand on our own Two Feet with Family and Friends

De-selfing means that too much of one's self (including one's thoughts, wants, beliefs, and ambitions) is 'negotiable' under pressures from the relationship.

Harriet Lerner, *The Dance of Anger*

The family/social phase, Wilber's fourth stage of development and first personal stage, is defined by individual development of rules and roles which mark our existence in relation to others; it is the level of family and social relationships. Because problems at this level are experienced as a fear of losing face, losing one's role and breaking the rules, recovery reveals our false coping patterns, such as compulsive reliance on substances or other addictive processes. In second stage recovery, we have to take this process to a deeper level where we look at unhelpful or unhealthy scripts from our family of origin or relationship that contribute to the pain underneath the addiction. We have to learn to replace these misleading scripts with an ability to stand on our two feet and be differentiated from our family and social relationships.

While the initial addictive process may have served as a misguided quest for wholeness, the person in stage two recovery is confronted by an underlying social anxiety; previously that anxiety was overcome, or at least managed, by chemical or neurochemical 'courage' from drugs, alcohol or compulsive behaviors which facilitated a sense of fearlessness, connection, belongingness and being in the groove. It is typical for recovering people to have to face underlying social anxiety which in the moment can be experienced as an almost pathetic begging for social acceptance, as if we have pinned a sign onto ourselves saying, "Please like me". We can constantly be in a state of watching others watch us, and perform in a self-conscious way, hoping to be met with social approval. The tragedy and vicious cycle of this pattern is that other people are loath to approve of people who are desperate for social approval.

Thus, the recovering person needs to learn how to directly risk being authentic in social and intimate relationships as exemplified by this clinical case example. Will, in recovery from alcohol addiction for about three years, was in counseling, working on freeing himself up to embrace all that life had to offer him in the present moment. As he started to let go of his past, it became clearer how he 'deselfed' himself in relationships.[1] It seemed Will was rarely in touch with his own essence and authentic beingness in interactions with friends and acquaintances. He gave up vital aspects of himself, including his feelings, perceptions and opinions, to please others. I pointed out to Will how he was constantly watching his external environment for cues to see how it was watching him. Because he felt that he had never fitted in socially, he was continually looking for external cues from others, and trying to give others what he perceived they wanted. In short, he was caught in self-consciousness and deselfing through his desire for guaranteed social acceptance. He was stuck in a pattern of desperately wanting external positive validation.

In our sessions, we worked together on this issue, and Will began to see that this constant watching and manipulating for validation was a form of begging and had become a stereotypical and limited habit, rather than a spontaneous and authentic response in the moment. This pattern of behavior kept him ill at ease and self-conscious, as acceptance from others was as unpredictable as the weather. Will began to see that if he dropped his begging, he could experience his essence directly. Rather than watching me or anybody else for cues of acceptance, Will could directly experience and express where he was coming from.

With this insight, Will began to make changes in his intimate relationship. He realized that he had fallen into a co-dependent pattern of trying to figure out and anticipate what his girlfriend wanted him to say, do or feel. He started to risk being true to himself by articulating where he was at. So rather than relying on his pattern of self-described "doting", he risked sharing his own emotions, including his anger and even setting boundaries by sometimes being able to say 'no'. He began to see that begging for acceptance actually resulted in the opposite, and disconnected him from his own self. To his surprise, these risky changes were met for the most part with approval from his girlfriend, who welcomed the direct expression of emotions and energy from Will.

Now, before we turn to ego identity level, I would like to demonstrate the work that can be done in social anxiety performance situations.

Social anxiety through time

Often social anxiety can be heightened with a performance aspect into an intense situation in which we continue to seek approval from others. For example, I made this journal entry when I first started teaching at a university fifteen years ago, as I wanted the students to like me and what I had to offer:

I woke up suddenly gripped by fear of what might happen a few hours later in my classroom. I could see myself starting my lecture, desperately clinging on to a self. I felt caught in my anxiety of trying to give a good lecture. Suddenly, I realized that there is no way that I could guarantee that the students would like my lecture, it was out of my hands. I silently said "screw it" to myself as I realized that nothing could be done. The energy seemed to go whoosh....into a vast stillness. I felt serene relaxation. And now at 5:30 in the morning, I could see clearly nothing could be done. Nothing could be done now, for the 9am lecture, so I relaxed back into my reverie waiting for the 7am alarm.

This journal entry described the pivotal insight I had in my first year of teaching at a university when I realized that I had to let go of trying to please my students and begging them to like me; instead, I could just share my own passion for the subject. It seemed that all I could do was prepare, and then let it all go. At least I could enjoy my own lecture. In these situations, it is something I always come back to: let it all go. Similarly, I noticed in my work with clients, it is something that they have to work on as well, letting go of trying to please the other, especially in social performance situations. We can get caught in fear and apprehension which we allow to warp our authentic expression of wholeness and joyful spontaneity.

Mindy had come to work with me because she had been experiencing some setbacks in her new masters program. She wanted to work on patterns of fear and anxiety which had been heightened by an upcoming major presentation to her graduate class. It was looming in one week. She found herself getting anxious about this presentation and had already spent a few restless nights.

"So, in this moment you are feeling okay, but then you think about your presentation and start to get anxious," I said to her. "Let us look into the nature of fear and anxiety. There is no way you can make the future secure. Psychological security is impossible. Doesn't the mind just come up with a bunch of strategies to make the future secure, but nothing really works as we try to be secure? You want to guarantee *now* that in a week's time people will really appreciate your presentation."

"The only answer is choiceless awareness in this moment as you realize there is nothing that the mind can do now to make a future moment secure. And when you give the presentation you will just have to let it all go, and enjoy yourself."

I watched Mindy to see if she could accept the invitation into choiceless non-judgmental awareness. Could she realize that all she could do was surrender now, and in the moment of her class presentation also surrender her begging for acceptance? A relaxed light of awareness came over her as she realized that there was truly nothing she could do in this moment, and all that she could do in the next moment or the moment of her presentation was to let go, and enjoy the moment without any judgment. She laughed with delight in her realization and resultant surrender. She saw that the fertile opportunity was always there to surrender and let go in this moment. We spent a few more minutes immersed in this realization before winding up the session.

We did not need another session as we spoke on the telephone and Mindy was feeling much more relaxed and in her groove after this. Her presentation went well and she ended up proceeding through her masters with flying colors, and soon after graduation she was hired as a family therapist. She confided to me six months later that she now realized that surrender can only happen one moment at a time; whenever she caught herself trying to make a future moment secure, she would let go to be choicelessly aware in this moment.

As this social level is worked out, and a person in stage two recovery learns to be authentic in articulating vital aspects of self, in social, family, intimate relationships and work, the core issue of ego identity can now be worked on in the next developmental level. Before proceeding to the next chapter, try the exercise below for standing on your own two feet.

Exercise 4: **Standing on your own two feet**

✳

We need to learn how to directly risk being authentic in social and intimate relationships.

> Imagine a social situation is that coming up where you find yourself socially anxious:
>
> Visualize yourself in the situation being anxious
>
> Notice that you are trying to be pleasing and gain approval from other people
>
> *See how hopeless and pathetic this begging for approval is*
>
> Now, just say to yourself, "Screw it"
>
> Let it all go
>
> *See how freeing it is to be in your own energy*
>
> Notice that in this moment all you can do is let it go
>
> *You realize you can only live one moment at a time*
>
> When the situation does actually come up, repeat the "Screw it" technique and let go
>
> *See that it is beyond your control whether somebody likes you or not*
>
> Stay in your own energy, be authentic, enjoy expressing yourself
>
> *See that you can handle whether somebody likes you or not*

Notice that authentic energy creates the chance of connection

See that is all you can do, be authentic in your own energy

Realize you are far better off being authentically you

Chapter 6: Deconstructing Ego Identity

You can never permanently recover from the dependent behaviors that have devastated your life without correcting the self-defeating thought patterns that keep you believing you are not good enough to handle problems and face painful circumstances on your own.

Tina Tessina, *The Real Thirteenth Step*

Ego identity

The next personal stage is ego identity, which represents the development of the mature ego. At this stage a person has a highly differentiated reflexive self-structure and has developed the capacity to reason, assert themselves and conceive of new possibilities for the future, based on their own desires, passions and intellectual capacities. Often in second stage recovery people still buy into an unhealthy underlying identity—a remnant of the time when they were immersed in addictive acting out—which may include false self-labels, such as 'addict', 'street smart', 'party animal' or the more negative 'loser', 'waste of skin'. It is at this stage that we may get caught in a narrow and confined sense of self, because these identity labels are a stultifying opposite of the spacious wholeness that is non-dual being. If we want to move forward beyond such a tightly conceived and egocentric view of existence, then now is the time to question narrow egoic identities, and see if a more expansive sense of self can be developed. This requires us to engage in a dynamic and active introspection and develop an expanding self-awareness. For instance, letting go of former egoic identities such as being a rebel or party animal seems obvious, and my experience in working with people is that this has typically already been done in early phases of recovery. Now, in the second phase of recovery, even the label of 'recovering addict' is seen to be too narrow an identity and now is the time to challenge that. As Bewley pointed out, some addicts in long-term recovery may actually require recovery from recovery.[1]

Bewley recommended Psychosynthesis,[2] a school of transpersonal psychology which gives us the tools to integrate various parts of the personality into great harmony through balancing and synthesizing. We can see the growth to a more expansive and inclusive self-sense in the following case example.

Cindy had been a drug addict for many years, but at the time of our sessions she had been in recovery for six years. She had hung onto her identity of being 'an addict in recovery' but was becoming aware of the narrowness and limitations of that label. In our sessions, we brought this whole identity into question. To do this, we looked at the essential archetypes that made up the client's journey.[3] As Cindy looked at her journey, she could see she comprised many archetypes, not just the 'recovering addict'. She was a 'helper,' a 'mother,' a 'lover,' a 'warrior' and a 'trickster', just to name a few.

We followed this with intense questioning and deconstruction. Cindy was tired of the addict label, and was quite ready to break out of the confines of this label, as she saw herself as a much more expansive person than that. We embraced self-questioning using my modified version of Byron Katie's four questions of inquiry.[4] The first question is "Is it true?" "Is it true that I am an addict?" Cindy of course said yes. The second question is "Is it absolutely true?" This question stumped Cindy because she could not say it is absolutely true because she knew that she was much more than that. It was too narrow. So she had to say, "No, not absolutely true." The third question is "What is it like when we believe in the story?" Cindy said she felt "limited, confined, labelled, diseased". I then asked Cindy the fourth question, "What is it like when you drop the story?" She immediately said, "I feel whole." We both laughed. She was moving beyond her narrow addict identity.

It was also evident that beneath the addict identity, Cindy was seeing herself as a victim. As we began to get in touch with a deeper sense of authentic self, Cindy was ready to challenge her identity of being a victim and see it as another way in which she was hanging onto a sense of a narrow ego identity. In responding to the question, "Is it absolutely true that you are a victim?" Cindy could see that it was not absolutely true. She had been hanging onto this victim identity, and creating crystallized stories about it. Because of all the work we had already done, Cindy was able to let this into her awareness. In looking at what aspects of her experience she was responsible for, Cindy sighed, and said that she had given up on herself early in her adolescence and stopped recognizing her own being. Instead, she had manipulated people through addiction and co-dependency patterns to get her addiction needs met. So, although she was not responsible for the abuse she suffered, she recognized the part she had played in setting this up. With this recognition, she seemed to come unstuck from her victim identity and became more in charge of her own life. Cindy's working through and letting go of attachment to archetypes—in her case the addict and the victim—had left her with a profound sense of deficient emptiness, in that she no longer knew who she really was. This deconstruction becomes an invitation to embrace the next level, existential issues.

We will now turn to look more fully at the existential level. Before that, take the opportunity to work on dropping an identity label or story and expand your identity.

Exercise 5: **Dropping identity labels**

✻

Work on a label or story of who you think you are. All labels and stories trap us into a narrow identity. For example, you could choose the label "I am a victim". You will use a modified version of Byron Katie's four questions of inquiry.

Choose a label or story you want to work on:

Make sure it is a label or story that you are preoccupied with

Ask yourself the first question "Is it true?"

Notice how the instant response is typically a yes

Ask yourself the second question, "Is it absolutely true?"

See how nothing is ever absolutely true, there are always exceptions

Ask yourself the third question "What is it like when I believe in this label or story?"

Feel all the emotions tied up with this label or story

See how this label or story makes you feel constricted and incomplete, not whole

Then ask yourself the fourth question, "What is it like when I drop the label or story?"

Feel the instant relief when you drop the label or story

See the spaciousness and wholeness inside

Realize you are not your thoughts and labels

Chapter 7: Being Authentic and Finding Meaning in the Existential Realm

They lack the awareness of a meaning worth living for. They are haunted by the experience of their inner emptiness, a void within themselves; they are caught in that situation which I have called the "existential vacuum".

Viktor Frankl, *Man's Search for Meaning*

Confronting existence

This level, the existential, is a powerful theme that runs through Western philosophy. Western existential philosophy has been preoccupied with questions of being and nothingness. The 19th century Christian existentialist Kierkegaard, in encountering his own existence, felt his existential anxiety or *angst* could only be truly resolved through religion.[1] Nietzsche, the early 20th century German philosopher, did not share Kierkegaard's enthusiasm for religion and declared "God is dead", urging humankind to live without any religious or metaphysical consolations.[2] French philosopher Jean-Paul Sartre felt that we live in nothingness and the only meaning humans can give themselves is the action to which they commit themselves.[3] The attitude of the existentialists of encountering existence through an act of self-created will has a certain value to humanity. It perpetuates a heroic outlook as each person must struggle to create meaning and accept anxiety as a fact of life. Leading existential psychologists Rollo May, Viktor Frankl and Irving Yalom recommended that the way to deal with the danger of being overwhelmed by the dark side of meaningless living, and by death and nothingness, is to find the will to meaning and the courage to be.[4]

At the existential level, the integrated body-mind confronts the reality of existence. To deal with an individual's encounter with existence, the existential perspective encourages authenticity, coming to terms with one's own finitude and mortality, fundamental self-responsibility, intrinsic meaning and self-resoluteness. At this level, people begin to confront the big questions of existence. *What is my life all about? What is my purpose for living? How to deal with the reality of death?*

We may have moments when our world collapses and we can find no firm ground. Nishitani, the Japanese existential philosopher, explained that in these moments a gaping abyss opens up the ground we stand on, and none of the things that have made up our life are of any use.[5]

I have faced the gaping abyss that Nishitani describes. I can remember in my own life, as I finished law school, and my one year marriage was crumbling, my whole existence was up for grabs. Everything had deconstructed and life had no meaning. I realized I had lived a false life because I had gone to law school merely to fulfill my parents' expectations. Now the whole world was collapsing around me as my fake career and a quick marriage had no meaning. Now, I was caught in the nausea of meaninglessness and the impending death of my former self and inauthenticity. This seems very similar to an addict's experience of hitting bottom and experiencing the total inauthenticity of the addiction lifestyle. A person's whole existence is deconstructed. Myself, I realized I actually wanted to be an existential-transpersonal psychologist. So, despite having full training as a lawyer, I knew I had to go back to university and get masters and doctorate degrees in psychology. I needed to live an authentic meaningful existence, I needed to live the life I wanted and follow my passion.

Working with people in second stage recovery involves the same invitation. An invitation is made to the person to begin to embrace an authentic existence. We will see how, although a person's partying days may be over, there can still be many remnants of an inauthentic existence, tattered rags of an old covering that need to be worked through in second stage recovery.

Morgan learns to live an authentic life
Morgan had been the classic jock basketball star partier and now he was a teacher in his late twenties, and a recovering sex and substance abuse addict. We got to the root of his inauthenticity in his second year of recovery and found the emptiness that was behind all the sexual acting out and partying. In short, because Morgan had kept himself busy with his acting out he had never really come to grips with the underlying hollowness. As he slowed down, he began to realize that at the heart of all of his acting out was an underlying existential depression, a crisis of emptiness, a collapse of his world. These were the inevitable result of an inauthentic existence, of a life lived on cruise control with a false embracing of life. But now his teaching contract was not being renewed for the next year, which gave such a jolt to his life that his world crumbled.

It was evident to Morgan that he could no longer live the way he did. Unconsciously, he had been living a death-denying (and therefore life-denying) unreflective life but now, in his existential crisis, he was confronting existence. Losing his teaching job opened up the reality of his own personal mortality. Suddenly his life was up for grabs and that meant he had to take his journey in life seriously. Now he had to find the courage to *be*.

As Morgan began to come at life from the perspective of being, he made two important decisions. The first one, related to times in the past when he had supported himself during summers with work as a bartender, and he decided that he could not do that any longer. Even though he was not drinking, it kept him in the addiction scene.

Secondly, related to this new emerging perspective of being, we began to look at how unconsciously and inauthentically he had approached his profession as a teacher. He had been a star basketball player at university and never tried very hard in his teaching classes, although he graduated, went on to a teaching job, and had worked for two years. As a teacher he had adopted a casual 'whatever' approach, but now he realized that this could no longer work for him. Now, suddenly, it seemed that the quest for self-knowledge was a priority. He knew that he would want to build that approach into his teaching as he grew in wholeness and authenticity.

This quest for authenticity was intensified when we sat in the reality of death in our sessions. This penetrated Morgan's almost unconscious Peter Pan sense of immortality. Together Morgan and I hung out in the reality of personal death. All of this was to help him move from an unconscious adolescent position to one filled with awareness.

Martin Heidegger, the German existential philosopher, talked about two modes of existence.[6] Firstly, there is the usual mode of a state of forgetfulness of being, which describes Morgan's previous condition. Secondly, there is a state of mindfulness of being in which one is continually aware of being, as one lives with the reality of death, responsibility and authenticity. This transition to the second level of being is of utter importance on the existential path, and it is a state that Morgan embraced. As existential therapist, Yalom, observed, the paradox of being is that "the idea of death saves us; rather than sentencing us to existences of terror or bleak pessimism, it acts as a catalyst to plunge us into more authentic life modes, and it enhances our pleasure in the living of life." [7]

As the existential reality of personal mortality and inevitable death came fully into Morgan's awareness, he truly discovered his own crisis of beingness and was inspired to embark on a quest to find what life was all about. He traveled extensively for six months and during this time he kept a journal and read some existential classics. Interestingly enough, getting in touch with questions of being and authenticity created a huge shift in Morgan's approach to his occupation as a teacher. He began to see that his own quest for beingness could be translated for the first time into an interest in the philosophy of teaching and how to connect with his students on the meaningful questions of life. For him, this lit the fire for teaching that had been so absent before. When he returned to teaching a year later this fire, this intensity, was mirrored back by his students. Morgan felt like a real teacher for the first time.

Discovering the limits of the existential perspective

Unfortunately, being authentic and finding meaning are not panaceas for all of the issues of life. We have discussed how the existentialist psychologists posited that existential freedom lies in choosing our attitude towards the fundamental prospect of annihilation and groundlessness. This perspective perpetuates a heroic outlook as each person must struggle to create meaning and accept anxiety as a fact of life. Yet, this perspective can be seen as a retreat from the problem of the encounter with groundlessness, nothingness and death. The emptiness keeps coming back. Randy, the counselor at the start of the book, had tried to live an authentic recovery existence working with addicts, but the ground of nothingness kept opening up inside him. An authentic existence doesn't resolve the basic issues of groundlessness and the abyss.

The crux of the problem is that we have both our apparent separate self egos and the emptiness. As Almaas pointed out this emptiness is "the gap between our essential nature and who we take ourselves to be. It is the great chasm separating our experience in the conventional dimension of experience from the fundamental ground."[8]

So, here we have the fundamental dilemma which I experienced in my own life. The ground of emptiness and disconnection kept opening up all of the time even though I was on an authentic journey. Bringing meaning to my life by getting a masters and doctorate in psychology and becoming a psychologist did not resolve the fundamental problem of emptiness. The emptiness kept coming back no matter what I accomplished. That emptiness did not care about the American Dream. The working out of emptiness became a fundamental issue in my own life and has deeply touched my work with people in recovery.

Running away from emptiness drives so much of the addictive life. In second stage recovery, the actual working through emptiness must be taken head on. Here, however, we are in for a huge shock. To make our home with emptiness we have to recognize and let go of our fundamental narcissism and separate self-sense.

I will now turn to describing my own journey of descent into emptiness and the concomitant unpacking and seeing through the illusion of the self. This involves a second descent at the end of stage two recovery. Before proceeding, you can check out your own awareness of death by doing the obituary exercise on the following page.

Exercise 5: The obituary exercise

*

Unconsciously up to now, we may have been living an unreflective and death-denying life, but now we can decide to consciously encounter existence and let in the reality of our own death.

> Write out on a piece of paper your own obituary that will run in the local newspaper:
>
> *Imagine that you have had the type of life that you wanted to live*
>
> Take your time writing out all of your achievements, passions, milestones and meaningful connections
>
> After finishing the obituary, let the reality of your death sink in
>
> *Realize you are alive right now*
>
> *Feel the preciousness of your life right now*
>
> *See how the awareness of your own death lets you take nothing for granted*
>
> Explore in the moment the feeling of being intensely alive
>
> *See how the awareness of your own death, lets you take more risks*
>
> Decide how you can most appreciate this sacred opportunity of life right now
>
> Commit to living an authentic and purposeful existence now

See what you need to do now to live the life you wrote about in your obituary

See that life is precious and death could be just around the next corner

Start doing what you need to do now

See that awareness of death allows you to be more authentic now

Life is precious

Part 2
Hitting Bottom in Second Stage Recovery: My Separate Self Addiction

Chapter 8: Discovering My Narcissism: I Am the Problem

The problem is that ego can convert anything to its own use, even spirituality.

Chogyam Rinpoche, *Cutting Through Spiritual Materialism*

Confronting my own narcissism

In my own recovery process, second stage recovery issues ended up turning me upside down; not only did I have to work on the intense issues we have already covered, such as the split mind, primal pain, social anxiety, letting go of stories and moving beyond ego projects, I was confronted with the one central aspect that tied all of this together, and that was that I was a narcissist. I was not a narcissist as defined by the DSM-V, but more a narcissist in the everyday sense of being preoccupied with self-esteem, the need for my specialness and uniqueness to be recognized, and having grandiose beliefs about my abilities.

"I want to be number one!" I remember screaming this during a primal scream workshop, early in my law school days. I thought nothing of it at the time but this fundamental narcissism remained a central problem of my existence. And the trap for me was that, even when I changed my gig of being a lawyer for being an 'awakened' transpersonal therapist, I kept my narcissism with me. Early in life I acquired the habit of very intense disciplined striving towards my goals, and kicking-in to an over-the-top state of intensity when needed. Now I used this same strategy for storming nirvana and the gates of enlightenment. This type of male warrior, conquering energy turned out to be very counter-productive in the awakening path.

I went through rounds of intense effort to climb what I thought was the supreme mountain of awakening. I thought heroic effort was what was called for, so that is what I gave. What I did not see at the time was how much this was all just efforts of the 'I', the individual seeker. There was the persistent 'I', the ego in the middle of all of these efforts, as if awakening and enlightenment were something that could be done, something that could be accomplished.

As I ripened on my own journey, I began to realize with a sense of irony just how much of a narcissist I still was. I had begun the path towards enlightenment not as a discovery process for truth, but for my own hidden egoic motivations. I could recognize in myself the 'spiritual materialism' of seekers that Chogyam Trungpa talked about. The tendency to collect spiritual experiences was actually in the service of the ego, a materialistic approach to spirituality.[1] The awakening journey was the ultimate trip of life for me, and it had a hidden narcissism built right into it from the get-go. It was the ultimate trip of establishing my specialness. I had been in law, but as soon as I heard about this enlightenment business, I was off and running. Slowly, it began to dawn on me after almost a couple of decades of seeking that 'I' was the problem, and not the solution. I began to see it was myself trying to go beyond the 'me' in this journey of awakening.

A darkness had come over my seeking. It was not an overnight transition, but gradually all of the exciting experiences of bliss, cosmic consciousness experiences, ecstasy and serenity started to lose their shine as I began to recognize all of these experiences were just temporary, and nothing really stuck. I was always searching, searching. I would find a new rock on the beach, thinking this new book or technique could be it; I would notice an energy upgrade for a while, but soon it would start to fade. I would then throw that rock back into the ocean, and walk down the beach, and then discover another rock, and then try that one for a while.

It became clear that I had tried just about everything: talk therapy, encounter therapy, bioenergetics, primal screaming, vipassana meditation, darkness meditation, long distance running, humming meditation, hollow bamboo meditation, self-inquiry, self-remembrance, letting it all go, surrendering—all worked for a while and then the intensity would fade. Nothing ultimately worked. The fantasy that I had for myself of being the intense quester who would find the gold at the end of the rainbow started to come into question. Was I just going around in circles? Despite my tour through the teachings of Osho and Papaji and others, both Western and Eastern, including Krishnamurti, Trungpa, Nisagardatta, Balsekar, Wilber, Adi Da, Almaas and Grof, the question: *Is there something wrong with my seeking?* began to haunt me.

What had started out so exciting, so blissful, so ecstatic and with so much promise, now had turned ugly and depressing. I was now mired in the garbage phase of my seeking and all of my grand desires had turned sour. I had started out looking for bliss, ecstasy and love, and now all I really had was pain, disillusionment and misery. I was on my knees. I was not the answer, I was the problem.

It was an unnerving revelation that all my efforts had been rooted in egoic grasping. The intense seeking of awakening, all the practices and meditations I had been doing, were part of my seeking trajectory that clearly led to the ugly gaping wound of narcissism. What was shocking to me was that, even in my stage two recovery and my quest for wholeness, I was still grabbing onto my specialness. So, with the emerging realization of my fundamental narcissism dressed up in spiritual clothing, I found myself in a descent which collapsed me out of my head and down into my guts, as my so-called specialness fell into the vast emptiness of being.

In the years since the shock of realizing that I was a total narcissist, and that it was me that was the problem, I have worked with many people on this fundamental issue of their central narcissism. For some, though, as with Cam, whose story I am about to tell, the overarching theme of narcissism can suddenly open up within them in an instant and a lifetime of narcissism can crash through in a few moments.

The falling star of narcissism

Cam had lived a life of turmoil. He felt he never really fitted in the game of life. He went through some difficult and dangerous situations, but he was a survivor, and managed to hang in there. He had a lot to deal with, from childhood trauma, to living on the streets, to addictions and mental health issues, to a failed marriage, and to a host of unsatisfying jobs. He took the plunge and finished university in his mid-forties, completing his social work degree just before he turned 50. Cam believed this would be a monumental achievement, a milestone in his life. To his surprise, he found that within a few days of graduating it seemed an empty accomplishment. This left him in a state of an identity crisis of meaninglessness and feeling caught in an existential vacuum. As the time seemed right, he did openly embrace an invitation to a non-dual workshop and registered for a non-dual conference set to occur a few weeks later.

Cam found the non-dual workshop to be intense and energetic, but he remained unsettled within his being. Despite a mounting sense of existential crisis and nihilism, he allowed a friend to co-opt him into attending the conference. At that time, he was in a low state, feeling quite desolate, as things were not working out for him as planned.

During the conference, however, he felt an intense swelling of energy inside himself that he could not explain. He found himself moved to joyous tears. Afterwards, with emotions perhaps intensified by the calamity of leaving his cell phone in a coffee shop the day after the conference, he was plagued by the burning question: *Who am I? Really?* The question seemed too hot for Cam's consideration at that time so he deferred it for a few days. Later in the week, he returned to it when he had a sudden epiphany about a tenant dispute over laundry access issues, an ongoing conflict he had been experiencing for over a year. Without warning, Cam abruptly understood how much he had been blindsided by his own self-interest regarding the conflict. When he came home that day, just moments after his insight about the laundry issue, he suddenly felt his whole world come crashing down on him as he revisited the question again: *Who am I?*

In that moment, for the first time, Cam could see that he had been a complete narcissist his whole life. Everything, even gestures of empathy and compassion, and feigning an understanding of narcissism, all of it was motivated by his own ego. This insight swept through him remorselessly and he felt as if the ground beneath him had turned into an abyss. He sensed himself plummeting through the abyss and, in the moment, his whole world changed as he actually saw the truth of his lifelong narcissism. Cam's life, filled with self-righteousness and self-interest, bloomed and crashed like a falling star. He felt completely changed. He got it! As he sat in a chair in his apartment, new insights about his life poured through him rapidly over the next several minutes.

This intense opening up of energy continued for the next few days. Cam felt he had so much energy it was similar to a manic episode. Unlike a manic episode, though, in this intense energy he could see that *he* was not the answer. He was one with the void and he was able to let go of a lifetime of misguided seeking and searching. This experience was shocking to him, as it did not come through effort but seemed to naturally sweep over him in a moment of true seeing. He found himself in a state of bliss and rapture, and almost surreal ecstasy for several weeks following this realization.

Whether it is a gradual dawning realization, as happened in my life, or a sudden realization like Cam's, the recognition that there has been a lifetime of narcissism can bring a person to their knees. In my own life, I found no way out but surrender. It took absolute hopelessness and failurehood to let go. We will look at these notions in the next two chapters. Check out your own awareness of narcissism with the following exercise.

Exercise 6: **Seeing your narcissism**

*

You are making a lifeline graph of all the ways in your life you have tried to be special up to now. This is designed to get you in touch with your long history of narcissism.

In the middle of a blank page make a horizontal line across the page, enter ages from 0 to your current age

Draw a vertical line at the 0 age point, make a vertical scale by numbering 1 to 10 above the horizontal line for the positive, and -1 to -10 below for the negative

Remember that narcissism experiences can be both positive and negative

Plot your various narcissism gigs of specialness on your graph at the age and the level from 0 to 10 of being positive or negative (the range is from -10 to +10)

See how you have a whole range of gigs with varying degrees of being positive or negative

If stuck, just remember the ways you have tried to be special, those are your gigs of specialness

Now, at your current age, plot the ways you are trying to be special now

See how it is harder to be aware of your present gig, as you are attached to what you are doing now

Look through your whole life and take in all of your gigs of specialness

See that in your whole life you have always been trying to be special, and the truth is that you are not special, but you are ordinary

In fact, see that your desire to be special is very ordinary

Look into your demand to be special

See how this demand makes you not the solution, as you have fantasized, but the problem

Let this in, "I am the problem"

Realize you can let go of this demand to be special right now

Let go of your need to be special and allow it to fall away

You can feel a giving up sensation, almost like a fist opening

Say to yourself, "I am ordinary"

Embrace your ordinariness

See how relaxed, humble and open you are when you are being ordinary

Chapter 9: Seeing Hope as an Addiction: Accepting Absolute Hopelessness

I am beginning to understand that this awakening is ruthless, stripping away every belief that I have ever held and ever clung to. Now there are no life rafts left, not even a piece of driftwood... My God. Things have got worse, not better. For previously there was hope.

Richard Sylvester, *I Hope You Die Soon*

Knowing that my seeking was all rot, I realized I could not cling onto these hidden fruits of narcissistic seeking anymore. All of this was just the separate self ego caught in a cycle of endless grasping. I came to a pivotal realization:

I woke up suddenly gripped by terror. I could see myself desperately clinging onto self, and trying to survive forever. It was a seeing that the self could try to survive for eternity but would forever live in fear of its own extinction. It was a profound feeling of terror, to face the fact that the self could be in total fear forever. I could plainly see that there was nothing to grab onto, nothing could be used to save me.

I had avoided the death of the separate self ego. I needed to die to my individual self. I had to give it all up. I needed to drown. Somehow, though, I kept hanging on. This led me straight to hopelessness.

My own embracement of hopelessness
I could feel myself stuck in a hellish, doom-laden swamp of seeking. What had began with so much promise of bliss,

realization and the fruits of awakening seemed to have turned into some sort of seeker's hell. All of the light and hype had turned into the pain of striving and suffering. A journey that had started out with so many dynamic aspirations had now fallen into hopelessness. I could see no way out.

Others have experienced this hopelessness in their seeking. Richard Sylvester likened this seeker's dilemma of hopelessness at the end of seeking to being stripped of everything and then left stranded with no resources:

> *In the story of time a year passed by during which I was very much in the desert and still felt separate but it was no longer felt in any way that meditation or psychotherapeutic processes or transpersonal techniques had any relevance anymore... You are without hope because it is seen that there is nothing that can move you forward. You are still unhappy but it's known now that there is no process which might bring about an end to your unhappiness. So there's no hope at all. Equally there is no help. There's no method which offers help and there's no person who can offer help. There's no belief anymore that for example sitting at the feet of the guru will somehow bring about an end to separation. The things that gave meaning to this life before are now seen to be meaningless. So hope, help and meaning are gone.* [1]

Understandings have flashed through and gone; techniques have been tried and abandoned as useless. Like Sylvester, here I stood in a place of profound hopelessness.

At first, I wanted to make this emerging hopelessness into a new strategy of hope. So, I set it up almost like a backdoor technique, a secret bargain: if I accepted hopelessness I would be delivered in some magical fashion, without going the whole way. After experimenting with this for a while, I realized that it still left me in the swamp of hopelessness.

I was trying to get somewhere or something out of this technique, and even though I could get an energy buzz for a while, I was soon back in a place of sterile hopelessness. It became clear to me that this was just an old form of seeking dressed up in new clothes. I was making a new technique called 'experiencing hopelessness'. It was another strategy of seeking, doomed from the get-go.

Hope is an addiction too

Thus, I knew that I needed to take hopelessness to a new level of unconditional acceptance. For me, contemplating this hopelessness and accepting it was an opportunity to let go of a lifetime's efforts. Such efforts were now revealed to be separate self-seeking, just more ego and a complete waste of time, leading only to misery and suffering. I found this to be an intense state in which to rest—and initially a very desolate experience: the end of hope. And I saw that all of the seeking had always been based on hope, hope for deliverance in the future. It was an addictive strategy to avoid the present moment and the hopelessness of the present moment. Hope had become my addiction: the answer was seen to always be just around the corner, but never here in the moment. To break the addiction I needed to accept the hopelessness of the seeker's dilemma.

Some spiritual teachers have called the situation truly one of unmitigated absolute hopelessness. As Chogyam Trungpa says:

It is a completely hopeless situation, absolutely hopeless. We do not understand—and we have no possibility of understanding anything at all. It is hopeless to look for something, to understand, for something to discover, because there is no discovery at all at the end, unless we manufacture one... Nobody is going to comfort you, and nobody is going to help you... There is no ground, so there is no hope.[2]

I could see how this hoping for something better in the future could go on forever. Accepting hopelessness, I, the burnt out seeker, needed to consider the total dissolution of seeking because what I was seeking was no longer contingent upon the hope of something happening or being done in the future. I could no longer expect a method or remedy to deliver me tomorrow. And embracing hopelessness could not be employed as a back-door strategy either. There is no bargain to be struck here. I was stuck in the present moment of hopelessness. I was here and now—trapped and hopeless.

So, there I sat in my absolute hopelessness, with no technique to practice, no strategy to put into play, in limbo with nowhere to go in the moment—and the moment was all I had. Hopelessness's twin sister, failurehood, showed up shortly after that, to finish off the one-two knockout punch to the separate self.

Before looking at failurehood in the next chapter, see if you can become aware of the hopelessness of your hope strategies with the following exercise.

Execise 7: **Accepting hopelessness**

✻

In this moment, you are going to look into and contemplate how you have tried to replace the hopelessness of your addiction with a hopeful strategy of recovery.

> Notice how you have been trying to win at recovery:
>
> Look and see how there is a self still hoping to win at recovery in the future
>
> *See that this is a deeper addiction, the addiction to the separate self*
>
> Notice all the strategies the self uses to try to win

Notice how the self moves from one strategy to the next

See how nothing works for long as the self keeps trying to perpetuate itself with all of its different strategies

Notice that, to deal with a looming hopelessness, the self looks to the future for hope

See how this has been going on for a long time and could keep going on forever

Notice how anything the self does to save the situation is just more self

See how any strategy of the self is hopeless as it is just strengthens the self

Notice the overriding feeling of hopelessness

Realize that nothing can be done

Accept the feeling of hopelessness

Say to yourself, "Nothing can be done"

Realize any strategy is just more hope

Do nothing

The situation is hopeless, and that is okay

Accepting hopelessness puts us right into this moment

Just be in this moment

Feel the relief of not needing to grab onto another strategy

Chapter 10: Embracing Total Failurehood: Existence Shows Up

Failure is the foundation of success, and the means by which it is achieved. Success is the lurking-place of failure; but who can tell when the turning point will come?

Lao Tzu

*She knows there's no success like failure
And that failure's no success at all*

Bob Dylan: "Love Minus Zero", *No Limit*

Embracement of total failurehood

I would like to say that the embracement of absolute hopelessness is all that I needed, and for many people that does the trick, but for me a sister realization was essential to finish me off: the realization of total failurehood. It was as if there had been a slippery 'I' still hanging on in some way, hopeless but with its teeth still locked onto me. Failurehood finished the job!

My story seemed very similar to that of the overzealous monk from this Zen story:

*During three years of severe training
Under the great master Gizan,
Koshu was unable to gain satori.
At the beginning of a special seven-day session of discipline,
He thought his chance had finally come.
He climbed the tower of the temple gate,
And going up to the arhat images he made this vow:
Either I realize my dreams up here,*

Or they'll find my dead body at the foot of this tower.
He went without food or sleep, giving himself up
To constant zazen, often crying out things like:
"What was my karma that in spite of all these efforts
I can't grasp the way?"
At last he admitted failure, and determined to end it all,
He went to the railing and slowly lifted his leg over it.
At that very instant he had an awakening.
Overjoyed, he rushed down the stairs and through the rain
To Gizan's room.
Before he had a chance to speak, the master cried:
"Bravo! You've finally had your day." [1]

Such a beautiful story! Like the monk in that story, despite all my efforts, awakening had escaped me. I had wondrous mystical experiences of cosmic consciousness, had been in rapture and blissfulness, had moments of 'liberation', and even accepted the hopelessness of my situation—but still something was subtly wrong. I was still hanging on in an underhand way to a sense of an independent, continuous self, fuelled by my desire for liberation. I thought somehow that I could keep that precious, very special 'me' and be an enlightened 'me'. I didn't understand how, if I relinquished myself, paradoxically I would become more spontaneously and freely 'myself' than I had ever been.

I could clearly see that all of my seeking had been a failure. I was laid bare with nothing to do, nowhere to go and no strategies to employ. After years of meditating, seeking, trying every version of a non-dual secret, finessing surrender, attaining, non-attaining, and employing every strategy under the sun, even hopelessness, I had reached a point of seeing that separate self seeking was a complete failure. This is the stage where we see that all this so-called spiritual work has been a mirage; we see that all efforts were dreams of the separate self. The separate self was trying to succeed at spirituality, trying to go beyond itself, while still hanging on to a central position in the apparent process. But, failure is inevitable because a separate self ego cannot succeed at awakening, despite all of its desperate efforts, because it's the problem not the solution.

So, in this place of absolute hopelessness and total failure-hood I sat, and realized I could do nothing to help myself. I was a total failure, despite all my successes. I could see it so clearly. And there was nothing I could do to stop seeking, as that would be just more seeking, seeking the end of seeking.

This new awareness seemed to touch on the edge of madness as I could see no way out of this mess. I could see clearly that nothing could be done. As Adyashanti explained:

> *So there comes a point where all techniques vanish, where anything that we've learned about how to re-adjust consciousness into a clearer state will fail us. Our techniques will be of no use. There will come a point in time when we will have to realize that there's nothing 'I' can do to let go at the existential level; there's nothing 'I' can do in order to surrender. Yet surrender and letting go are absolutely what is called for.*[2]

It is here at this crossroad that the stage is set for the falling away of the seeker to reveal the oneness of existence that was already the case.

Giving up: letting go the goal of awakening

In my own experience the day arrived when I became so exhausted that I just gave up. I realized that there was nothing I could do. Everything I did was wrong because it was me doing it. Giving up just happened. But—and at last—this was not something that was done as a technique. At that moment, I clearly understood that it was not in my control. Before I reached this point, I had tried everything under the sun on my journey but nothing was permanent, nothing was securely the same, because it was all just 'me' and my egoic grasping for something outside, something beyond, somewhere different.

I could see in the moment that there was no actual enlightenment or awakening in existence; they were just concepts. I had tried to attain awakening as if it was a state or goal out there, at which I could arrive. I saw the futility of pursing an object, even enlightenment or awakening, as this meant I was always striving, trying to attain. There was no rest, no ease, no spontaneous beingness without judgement. Giving up the goal of enlightenment and awakening put me right back into the present moment so I could see what actually was. In letting go, I am passive and available to existence—no longer demanding, searching and seeking. In giving up, I let go of my effort and am open to existence. So, in the moment with absolute hopelessness, and total failurehood, and letting go of the goal of awakening, I am truly at the end of the line. I have tried everything, and nothing has worked. I realize that my holding on has only been prolonging the misery. Here, one can see that it is time for the death of the self, which has been hanging on for a long time.

No escape

I could see that all of this seeking was an attempt to escape the present situation. As with any addiction, I was always looking for a way out. And now I could really see the futility of the escape strategy, as it never allowed me to accept just *what is*. This became my invitation: to accept *what is* with no desire for change.

Nowhere to go but this here and now. Stop trying to change the situation. In a subtle way, all of my effort had been based on escaping and finding a sanctuary. But, instead, can I accept being here? Can I stop striving to escape and accept this situation? I knew the answer; it was to accept existence in the moment. So, in this moment, with no desire to change it, I sat.

Here I was, at the end of the line. It seemed as if I was 'done' as there was nothing left for the self to do, no technique to practise, no book to read. I just dropped into utter effortlessness. More accurately, I fell down into effortlessness. I watched timelessly as my separate self went down quietly, without splashing around, and was silently submerged into the ocean of existence. Things were over for 'me', and I sat calmly in this place where 'I' was no more. All of my efforts, frantic seeking, and the whole 'me' had nothing to do with this, as all of this 'me' seemed to all just drop by itself. It was as if I could see a big black Titanic ship of effort falling into the horizon of the ocean, and slipping into the ocean forever, gone. All the effort of this lifetime gone, gone, disappeared...

Through darkness to light: dissolving into the void

With the falling down of all effort and the abandonment of 'project me', there was just non-existence, blackness, a black void of extinction, the valley of the shadow of death. Everything was swallowed up into non-existence. I made no effort to escape, just merging and letting go into the black void. I had been extinguished! What remained was the vast, utterly still, black darkness of eternal non-existence—a vast, still ocean where nothing is. Who could have known that this absence experience could be so awesomely and hauntingly beautiful?

Sitting in the black void felt almost like an eternity, but it was only probably a few moments of measured time. And then the blackness transformed into a brilliant dazzling light. I looked around and laughed, I could see eternal existence itself... lit up as brilliant vast translucent stillness, the eternal interconnected light, the suchness of existence. The hidden splendor had revealed itself without the familiar 'me' in it. This was very strange because it was not something I had done.

It was so simple, "This is it!" I laughed at the ridiculousness of the whole seeking game, as I could see all of existence is already enlightened, and we all are already there where we are trying to get to.

No past, no future, just this moment. The whole journey had been a mirage as the light of non-dual being was always already here, already present, from the beginning. Spiritual growth and seeking were part of a grand illusion as there was no place to go. All my efforts were in fact an avoidance of *what is*, as it is. It had all been a ridiculous affair. So, here I sat in absolute hopelessness and total failurehood, with nothing to do, and nowhere to go, and here in this moment, it is obvious, it is all here. The realization is 'just this'. So, the search took me on a wild goose chase only to eventually deliver me back to the moment. And ironically, I could clearly see, it was all right here.

Just this moment, just this, nothing more is needed but an embracement of this. There is nothing to grow towards, there is nowhere to get to, there is no goal. To think of goals has been a complete waste of time. The whole time I was already there where I wanted to be. I was trying to do the impossible task of reaching where I was already at—a sure recipe for madness!

And in the moment, I could clearly see there is no self. In the light of existence, in non-conceptual awareness, there is no self. In this moment, I am connected with all of existence but there is no separate self. I look within and cannot find the self anywhere. I look all around outside, and in this place of spacious expansion, no 'I' exists.

Here in this moment it is obvious, I see the tremendous overflowing of existence and it is all here. The miracle is this. And as I sit in my chair, it is clear that all is here, the total vastness of existence, and it is all here in this moment in form and formlessness. I had been so desperate to get there, I had not realized it was already here all of the time, always already here. And now, the seeker's feeling that something is not quite right is gone, as I realize it is all okay right here, right now.

What is so clear is that it has always been here and is already complete. My efforts to possess and grasp it only got in the way. Because it is already here, it just needs to be re-realized and lived. And so, this leaves us right here, right now. People try to reach, and in their striving they continue to miss the mark. As Tony Parsons keeps emphasizing, the open secret is "All that is is this right now, and this is the infinite expression—there is no other."[3] So, the search took me on a long journey only to eventually deliver me back to this moment. This seems tragic if we are still in the dream of seeking, but very funny when the open secret of existence is revealed.

Check out the transformational freedom of your own seeker's failurehood on the following page.

Exercise 8: **Accepting total failurehood**

※

In this moment see if you can accept the total failurehood of the self so that the illusion of 'you' trying to succeed falls away.

> Remember how you realized the failurehood of your addiction:
>
> Now notice how in recovery there is still a self trying to recover and succeed
>
> *See that this is a sign of a deeper addiction, the addiction to self*
>
> Look at all the ways the self has tried to succeed at recovery
>
> *Realize all of the attempts to succeed always end up in failure*
>
> Look at all the ways the self has even tried to go beyond the self
>
> *See that this always results in failure as the 'me' can't go beyond the 'me'*
>
> Let it in, "I can't succeed at dropping the self"
>
> *See that there is nothing you can do*
>
> Accept the total failurehood of your self
>
> *See that hanging on to trying is futile*
>
> Give up trying
>
> *See how relaxing it is to give up effort*
>
> Enjoy this moment

Accepting failurehood leaves you open to this moment
You are free to embrace what is

Part 3
Accelerating the Surrender Process

Chapter 11: Using Almaas' Transformation of Narcissism

The structure of self-identity begins to be revealed as a psychic structure patterned by images from past experience. Further experience increasingly reveals the unreality and underlying emptiness of the central self-structure.

A.H. Almaas, *The Point of Existence*

I realized that I could not expect the people I worked with to go through the madness of journeying through the swamps of narcissism, hopelessness, failurehood and the black void in exactly the same the way I did. Consequently, I was delighted to find the work of A.H. Almaas, which lays out the fundamental problem of narcissism inherent in addiction and the human condition and a process for transforming this narcissism into the realization of being. Almaas' model mirrored my own experience of the addiction to the separate self and the transformation of narcissism so completely that I have been able to use it intensely in my work with clients and students, as it lays out a clear framework and a process which is easy to follow.

Fuel for the addictive pathway is not only found in manipulation and escape from pain, but also much deeper, in the belief in a separate individual existence and its accompanying narcissism and grandiosity. As in my own story, it is essential that the underlying narcissistic mindset and behaviors of the addicted person are addressed and worked through. As people proceed in recovery, the process is no longer just one of emotional repair, but now must be a deconstructive one. This involves facilitating the falling away of narcissism and falling into true being, so that an authentic surrender in recovery can happen. We are looking at a wholeness that is more than emotional healing and integration but moves beyond the self into non-separation and, as Jess later on in this chapter found, 'a total loving presence in this moment'.

Almaas' transpersonal model of facilitating the transformation of narcissism and ego death is particularly helpful because it provides a means by which typical issues such as ego preoccupation and narcissistic grandiosity can be worked through. With its primary focus on moving away from reliance on the false egoic self and relaxing into essence, this model highlights the pivotal issues in transitioning from stage two recovery to wholeness, embracing non-dual being and stage three recovery.

Before exploring this model in more depth, it will be helpful to further examine and remind ourselves of the role of the egoic narcissistic self that is a central aspect of addiction. The transformation from addiction is not limited to correcting behavior or reconstructing a healthier, more positive sense of self. What is needed is more than the integration and psychological wholeness sought through Western psychology. The wholeness of non-separation and seeing through the illusion of the separate self must be rediscovered.

Recovery rests upon dismantling or seeing through the illusionary nature of the egoic narcissistic self that drives the addiction. On the periphery of experience, the various strategic forms of manipulation and deception keep the addictive personality alive, and yet, when confronted and deconstructed, what one has taken as the self is seen to be a mere pretense. The felt sense of individuality is made up of a collection of thoughts, beliefs and memories, held together through fixated awareness around the 'I' thought.

The paradox is that one comes to believe he or she exists as a separate individual, but the moment awareness turns in on itself to locate this so-called separate self, it cannot be found. The 'I' thought dissolves back into emptiness. It does not mean becoming less than we were, and this will become clear as we take this exploration further.

People who are caught in addictive pathways, do not deconstruct the 'I', but hang tightly onto their form of unique specialness. We mentioned at the outset that Carnes has a poignant description of the narcissistic sex addict which can easily be extended to most people caught in most addictions. He refers to them as the 'Master of the Universe' personality. This person can't tolerate the threat to his or her own existence and so avoids the realization of the illusion of the separate self and the façade of specialness at all costs:

> *The Master of the Universe theme emerges in addicts' lives in many different ways. But constant is the rationale that all is justified because of the addict's uniqueness, specialness, or superiority. In their addiction, they are set apart from others, either made of "the right stuff" or having some special right or need others don't have. Being out of control requires that you have no limits.* [1]

In explaining this notion, Carnes cites a central theme of classical drama; the hero often comes to grief because of one flaw, which is hubris, or excessive pride and arrogance.

The belief in separation is the antithesis of wholeness; it leaves us bound up in confusion and tension, always having to defend ourselves against the unpredictable rhythms of existence. Identification with the mind, the 'I' thought, can be seen as the original seed of misery and suffering. The 'I' thought grasps at external seeking to justify and bolster its existence. It is here that Almaas's transformation of narcissism approach can be used to great effect. For the person in recovery, still caught in the Master of the Universe script, the grasping onto specialness can be dissolved in the intensity of beingness in the present moment. Realizing our true nature is to re-orient awareness back to the present moment, to our original ordinary condition of simple abiding presence. The need to be a somebody, to be mirrored in a special way, to be seen and appreciated, is a defense against being merely, but delightfully, ordinary or nothing at all. Deep within the core of our being is a vast empty spaciousness untainted by the toxic ingestion of addictive behaviors. In this spaciousness, there is an absence of the egoic self. The problem is that this absence is perceived as a lack, a death in fact, and therefore, an experience to be avoided at all costs.

What is called for here is radically different from our usual strategy of protecting the little construct of 'me'; it is a letting go of egoic self, and a fall into the vast ocean of being in which no independent egoic 'I' exists.

This letting go is inherently available to all of us human beings, but the veils of narcissism obscure our true nature. Thus it is critical for any individual willing to move beyond the personality of an addict to deconstruct his or her narcissism and the concomitant Master of the Universe mindset.

Almaas has outlined a simple approach for this, which mirrors the stages I went through in my own life, and I have been able to use this approach to assist clients in transforming their narcissism. This approach synthesizes the schools of modern depth psychology with the spiritual domains of human consciousness. It recognizes self-realization as the ultimate endeavor of all sentient beings, the pinnacle of human consciousness, where the personal and impersonal aspects of consciousness are fully realized and the sense of individual self-hood is exposed as illusionary in nature. Eighteen steps of transformation are identified in an unfolding stage-like process, where each step represents a significant experience of the dissolution of personality.[2] For the purposes of simplicity, I will condense the eighteen steps to six essential steps for deconstructing the narcissistic identity of an addict.

They are:

1. Fakeness and the empty shell
2. The narcissistic wound and rage
3. The great betrayal
4. Ego activity
5. The fall into the black chasm of being
6. Realization of essential identity

Now let me show how I used Almaas' model in working with Jess, a recovering sex addict.

Jess's transformation of narcissism

Jess, now in his mid-thirties, had been down a long and twisted ten-year road of internet pornography, massage parlors, escort agencies and prostitutes. This life trajectory was especially perplexing for him as he had been trained as a social worker. Subsequent to this training he had switched careers and completed a film studies degree, but after job offers in the film industry dried up, he was employed as a forklift operator at a plant. Jess had been in recovery from sex addiction for four years, and regularly attended an SA group in his town of residence.

In our first session he complained to me that even after four years he was still 'white knuckling' it, in that he still had lots of cravings, and even occasional relapses. It appeared to me that, in many ways, he seemed to be caught in a stalled second stage of recovery, the equivalent in sex addiction of the dry drunk phase of the alcoholic. He had stopped sexually acting out except for periodic slips into internet pornography.

However, his recovery had not progressed for years. Jess seemed perplexed by this as he had worked with many counselors, had been a regular attender at SA meetings, and even recently was a charter member of a new group. Additionally, over the years, he had not just worked on stopping his acting out, but he had gone further to deal with issues of trauma and being more connected to his feelings. Yet, here he was looking across the counseling room at me, claiming frustration at how stuck he was.

Fakeness and the empty shell
In our first session after hearing his story, I proposed to Jess that maybe he was stuck because he had not really worked on the root issue of his sexual addiction, which was his underlying narcissism. Exposing the empty shell of the narcissistic ways of the addict is a critical first step in becoming whole and awakening to one's true nature. As we have already discovered, lies, deceit, manipulation and control are aspects that keep the Master of the Universe personality in place. This personality structure is likened to that of an empty shell because, without the sexualized mirroring, it begins to thin out and dissolve. When the patterns of manipulating the other for sexual conquest and validation are addressed, the fakeness is exposed. What is revealed here, instead of a self with inherent substance and inner richness, is an impoverished empty shell that feels insubstantial, false and vacant.

I invited Jess to look at the whole pattern of his sexualized acting out, including all of his hidden intense fantasies. As we processed the behavior and the fantasies, it was clear that both were driven by a whole pattern of yearning for specialness and the idea of being a god-like Master of the Universe, beyond the rules and values of 'ordinary' people. He felt that people should recognize how special and wonderful he was, and mirror back to him that he was the special one, giving him anything he wanted sexually.

I asked Jess how long he had been special, and he said, "Since I was a little boy. My family thought I was a little Jesus." I asked him to think of himself going to a convention in which there were thousands of people like him who thought they were spiritually special, and that they wanted to get their sexual desires fulfilled. I chuckled with Jess and said, "There must be hundreds of thousands, maybe millions of people like that. How ordinary is that?"

Jess sat there stunned. He could actually see the reality of what I had said. It was an intense realization. His Master of the Universe gig had been exposed. Funny, it was actually a very ordinary gig, nothing special at all. I invited Jess not to defend against this experience but to allow it in its entirety. When a person ceases to resurrect the empty shell through continued acting out or fantasizing about their specialness, there is an opportunity to fall deeper into being. Firstly, though, the narcissistic wound with its characteristic rage has to be fully exposed and worked through.

The narcissistic wound and rage

As the empty shell is exposed, an underlying pain begins to emerge—the pain of the narcissistic wound. It is often intense, with an anguish that seems intolerable and a grief which seems bottomless. Here, we have to directly confront the constricted and limited situation from the vast, expansive and dynamic perspective of beingness. It must be seen for the first time that we have been living on the mirroring from others to fuel our separate and limited personality and reinforce our need for specialness. Now, as that validation from the other is taken away, along with the so-called specialness, we are confronted with our own gaping narcissistic wound.

The wound, however, is not created by the loss of support from being mirrored by the outside world, but more from having lost contact with our own essential nature in the first place. We see, perhaps shockingly, just how much life energy has been spent in supporting an illusion. This crisis of being is one of the reasons for relapse in early recovery. As the sex addict disengages from sexual mirroring, the resulting spiritual crisis can be intolerable. The rage that simmers and erupts is a reaction to the wound and can be seen in the addict who sabotages their recovery process through projection and blame—which is at root no better than supporting the illusion of a special self by the mirroring of others. Attempting to bypass this wound simply prolongs the suffering. The only remedy is to accept, understand and go through the pain; to step into the eye of it without the desire for escape; to allow it to wash through one's entire being.

As I processed this with Jess, it was as if the gaping wound had been opened up. He was mad. He admitted he had thought there was a special plan for him, that he truly was a gifted person on a very important spiritual mission in life. He was now very disillusioned with this plan and felt that God and existence had screwed him over. I invited Jess to embrace his narcissistic rage. Using the empty chair technique, we put existence itself in the empty chair and I encouraged Jess to let existence have it. With a little encouragement from me, he was soon screaming loudly and catharting out his anger at existence. He was livid that he had been let down by life, and even screamed obscenities at God in the empty chair.

After he had exhausted his rage at existence and God, I sensed there was another sore spot, so I invited Jess to process his rage against females. Off he went again, railing against the empty chair, angry that females had not recognized how special he was and how they had refused, for the most part, to be willing participants in his sexual fantasies and acting out. He spewed rage for ten minutes, and finally collapsed back into the chair. Ironically, after venting his rage, Jess was now more present and open than he had been for quite some time. We proceeded to the next stage.

The great betrayal

Helping Jess to work through his gaping narcissistic wound and his rage set the stage for an even deeper insight to be revealed; that of the great betrayal. This betrayal is not about feeling betrayed by others but is greater than that; it is one of self-betrayal: we chose people in our environment and their approval over our own essence. The recognition of our own betrayal puts us in a seemingly bottomless pit of pain, in which there is great sorrow, regret and even shame, guilt, and self-hatred.

What is most critical here is not the realization that we were betrayed by others, but that we betrayed ourselves in our futile attempts to establish our specialness through manipulating those others. I asked Jess, "Can you see that all of this sexual acting out was you just trying to be the answer? You betrayed yourself." At this stage it is vitally important for the client to allow this realization into conscious awareness so that the victim psychology can be shattered; there is an end to the 'poor me' mindset, which projects onto others and blames them. So, I just sat there with Jess, waited, and let him be with this dilemma. He had to see for himself that it was he himself who had chosen the fake world of one night stands, massage parlors, internet pornography, sex chat lines and the conquering sex mentality. All of this was part of his Master of the Universe specialness that he was hanging onto. He did it to himself. It only took a few minutes. Suddenly, his eyes lit up, and he laughed and said, "I have been a complete total narcissist." With this powerful insight the pain had been replaced by humor. As he sat there, clearly something relaxed in him. It was as if he let go of his narcissistic specialness, and fell into beingness. Jess reported, "This is strangely relaxing."

Here, we see the great paradox of the realization of the great betrayal. In trying to survive, we sacrificed our own essence. This realization, as Jess has shown, frees the person to fall into being as the person sees it is they themselves who are responsible for the betrayal of self. A side-effect of this is that we may find that our sense of self in the body is no longer located in the head but is shifting to our heart, our belly and our breathing.

Ego activity
The collapse into being came at the end of this session and it was as if Jess had been stopped in his tracks. Seeing the magnitude of his own betrayal of beingness and essence had shifted him back into the vulnerability and defencelessness of the present moment. I invited Jess to rest in this natural open and vulnerable beingness state for a few minutes as we wound up our session. His homework was to be just in this place of beingness with no grasping onto specialness. In a way, this homework was a set-up. I knew the narcissism of the ego and mind, does not permanently give way so easily. I expected Jess to have to confront increased awareness of ego activity in the next week.

When he returned, Jess reported how hard it was to stay in this vulnerable open place. Embracing the present moment is an invitation to the death of the egoic separate self, and the mind will raise hell at this point. The new stillness feels like death, and the egoic self reacts frantically by intensifying its activity in a frenzy of feverish agitation and inner obsessiveness. Although this type of ego activity can occur at any stage of unfolding, it is intense here, because the underlying emptiness is perceived directly and identified as a threat. We may even try to defend against the emptiness by reverting to old addictive behaviors which are perceived as having lesser consequences.

Jess reported that in the past week he had noticed how his mind and ego frantically looked for ways to prop himself up in the old familiar way. He had even briefly looked up some internet porn but shut it off after five minutes, realizing how hopeless it was. Other than that, he was consumed all week by a sense of feeling lost and out of place, that he needed to put himself back together. I wanted Jess to recognize that all his activity, including sexual fantasies and acting out, was merely a desire to escape his own inner emptiness and dread of the "big black hole" he could feel in the bottom of his belly. I asked him if he was willing to work on this fear of the underlying emptiness with me in the session. He hesitantly agreed.

The fall into the black chasm of being

Firstly, I reminded Jess that he had dropped into his beingness during our last session, so he had already done this before. Next, I invited him just to relax and breathe into his belly. He then reported that he felt like he had contracted upon himself and was now suspended over a black abyss, which he could crash into and hurt himself if he let go. The abyss did not have the presence of a soft loving holding energy, but he sensed it as more like a wall.

I encouraged him just to stay with the awareness of his belly, but now to let go of any judgment of the situation. He was to have no choice or preferences, just be at one with the situation. I encouraged him to accept *what is*, instead of trying to frantically save himself in some way.

As we sat in our chairs, he continued to feel himself clinging and contracting over the black abyss, as if he could be smashed by the impact of hitting bottom. Again, I invited him to just relax into the abyss with no judgment, as the deep abyss was in fact his own energy. It is what Almaas called the 'loving black chasm of being'.

As Jess sat there, it was clear from his expression that he had stopped fighting to protect himself, and he was now just letting go. He felt that he had broken through something and now was resting in a blackness; a blackness that for him was strangely transforming. As he continued to breathe into the blackness, he indicated that the energy was no longer a black coldness but had a loving spaciousness to it. This was something very new to him; the vastness of inner spaciousness. We sat there in the meditative stillness of the moment and he reported, "It's like an inner ocean of energy has opened up for me."

Here, Jess was embracing the vastness of being with no separate self to hang onto. As he relaxed into it, he experienced that in his vastness he was truly okay. Almaas described this remarkable experience:

> *In the black space we are aware of the absence of the sense of self... It is a nothingness, but it is a nothingness that is rich, that is satisfying precisely because of its emptiness. It is a direct sense of endless stillness, of pure peacefulness, of an infinity of blackness that is so black that it is luminous. It is a transparent blackness that is radiant because of its purity. This is not the experience of a self, an observer beholding the endlessness of space; rather, it is the experience of the self experiencing itself as the infinity of peaceful space.*[3]

This is a radical transformation, where our familiar center of self shifts from working hard to stay in a place of narcissistic addiction to falling into non-dual being. Abidance as pure black emptiness burns up the seeds of separateness and the grasping for a point of self-referencing collapses completely. Here, we make our home in the spaciousness of being, devoid of any points of reference, free from the snares of desire and fear, and we recognize that freedom was always available, here and now, in the ordinariness of the moment.

Jess seemed pleasantly shocked by his transformation. I invited him to continue to make this vast open beingness his home in each moment over the next week. For homework, I specified that he should keep being in his no judgment place of choiceless awareness and accept *what is*. I was aware that living in the vast openness of being can be terrifying for the mind, and Jess needed to be mindful of the mind's attempt to move away from the vulnerability and insecurity of open beingness with no ego to hang onto. I encouraged him to watch the mind's attempts to find a way to settle back into the ego and the 'I'. For Jess, this included not judging his state of boredom. While having had moments of ecstatic beingness in session, he also had a pattern of returning to feelings of boredom and negative nothingness outside of session. He needed to learn to be with the emptiness, without judgment, and without trying to change *what is*.

Realizing essential identity

When Jess came back the following week, he reported feeling he had made substantial progress in moving from a sense of deficient emptiness to resting in a fullness and wholeness of being. He found the level of ego activity had been quite stilled.

As Jess shared his progress over the past week, I encouraged him to wrap up his description and let go of describing anything about the past week, as it had passed. I invited him rather to be completely present in this moment. Jess took this invitation to surrender to this moment easily, and I noticed him drop into silence and full presence of being. He had been able to get the knack of letting go into the present moment and was flowing along. He laughed with me at how easily this had happened.

I asked Jess to describe who he was in the moment, and he replied, "I am this vast consciousness, this vast space. I used to think it was nothingness, but now I see it is a full nothingness. It is like a total loving presence in this moment." I nodded in agreement.

Later in the session Jess also described something very interesting. During the week and in this session, he felt himself in an ecstatic beingness that he had never experienced before. Along with this, he reported that it felt as if his masculine side and feminine side were coming together in the moment. It was like a sacred union. The energy of existence was flowing through him, with nothing blocking it—he felt that he was experiencing a cosmic connection.

In the experience of bliss and ecstasy, and the cosmic connection with existence, his perspective on his sexualized mindset shifted. He laughed to himself, realizing that he was already in a place of wholeness. Now, his reaching out for conquest, orgasm and release no longer made sense to him. He was already whole. He could also clearly see what I had tried to explain to him in an earlier session about the fixation on grasping onto his desires. Previously, right up to the last week, when he noticed an attractive woman he would feel a sexual desire, then grasp onto it, and almost hoard it for later. Now he realized that he could just notice the attraction, and then let it fall away. He did not have to hang onto it, because he was no longer using sexual desire and sexual fulfillment to try and get somewhere else, or to be anything other than his authentic self. He could just stay in the energy of the present moment. He now saw clearly that his sexual acting out and fantasizing was a way for him to grasp outside himself for support. By being choicelessly aware he realized that he could notice beauty in the moment and did not have to hang onto it.

Jess and I only had a couple of follow-up sessions after that. Life had definitely shifted for him. He reported that working on his narcissism had transformed his recovery, and he no longer was stuck in the second phase. Instead he could feel himself embracing wholeness. He continued with active involvement in Twelve Step meetings and worked his recovery, but life actually felt like it was moving ahead for him now after a few years of being stuck. He was enjoying new possibilities of a promotion at work, and a slowly progressing new relationship.

Jess's case shows the transformational opportunity available by loosely following the process laid out by Almaas. It seems essential that a person has to become aware of, to fully admit and let in to their consciousness, the fakeness and empty shell of their narcissistic pursuits of specialness, so that the fall into being becomes a possibility. You can explore letting go of your narcissistic façade with the following awareness exercise.

Exercise 8: **Transforming narcissism**

✳

In this moment see if you can let go of your narcissism.

> Get in touch with a feeling of the fakeness of your narcissistic gigs
>
> Notice how the body feels like an empty shell
>
> *Feel the patheticness of your narcissism*
>
> Notice the wound inside as your specialness is being threatened
>
> *Sense how gaping this wound is*
>
> Notice how you might want to defend against this awareness of your fakeness and your wound
>
> *See your defensiveness, how you want to lash out and blame others for taking away your specialness*

See the tendency to want to reconstitute your narcissism

Resist going with this ego activity of rebuilding your narcissistic specialness

Now take it further, by doing a second part:

Look through your whole life, and notice how it was you yourself who sold out your essence

See if you can see the greatest betrayal has not been done by others, but by yourself to yourself, as you sold out to others to ensure survival or for approval and validation

Watch again for ego activity that will try to defend against this realization

See if you can just accept this realization, "I betrayed myself"

Now watch how accepting this realization breaks up the narcissistic façade

It may seem like you are falling out of your head down into your heart and your belly where you breathe

Notice that you are okay even if your identity or sense of who you are has dropped out of your head into your heart and belly

Try to bring awareness to the feelings in your heart and to your belly as you breathe in and out

Realize this is a new way of being for you and it might take a while to get used to it

Notice any judgments that come up in the moment

Say to yourself, "No judgment"

See how it is much easier if you do not fight or judge the experience

Just relax and be with *what is* in awareness in the moment

Notice that you may have a sense of an 'I' defending against what might feel like a black hole or abyss in the belly

See that you are separating 'I' and the abyss in the moment

Let 'I' and the abyss become one, say to yourself, "I am the abyss"

See if you can merge with the abyss with no fight and no judgment

Give up trying to save yourself, let go of grasping onto the 'I'

Feel the relief you get by stopping any effort to save yourself

You are one with the abyss

See that being one with the abyss allows it to expand and transform

Notice how staying with the abyss, it transforms from blackness to a translucent light

You have come home

You are this vast spaciousness

You are this loving beingness

Chapter 12: Letting Go of Being Saved by the Other

I am not out to liberate anybody. You have to liberate yourself, and you are unable to do that. You see, I am in a very difficult position. What I have to say will not do it. I am only interested in describing this state, in clearing away the occultation and mystification in which those people in the "holy business" have shrouded the whole thing.

U.G. Krishnamurti, *The Mystique of Enlightenment*

As we look deeply into our recovery and awakening journey and start to see the illusion of the separate self, a parallel realization can hit us: we have been playing a game of trying to let go of the self by trying to be saved by the 'other'. This over-reliance on the other can be a powerful obstacle on the path to embracing third stage recovery and non-dual being. While reliance on the other can initially be very helpful in the short term, over time it can be an enacting of the central object relation between the central ego and the ideal other, which we look to, to be comforted, satisfied, fulfilled and nourished. These perceptions are not founded on reality. We are still living in a projection of the other, which started with mother or a primary caregiver when we were a baby, and then we looked to father, a secondary caregiver, a teacher, a coach, a lover, a friend, a mentor, a guide. With each, we wanted to be taken care of and soothed. So even as we start to deconstruct the self, we may still be inadvertently trying to be saved by the other. It is the old addictive pattern of trying to comfort our inner state by reaching out to a ritual or process to make ourselves more comfortable; here the reaching out is to another idealized person such as a spiritual teacher, or indeed a therapist, healer or shaman.

Almaas captured the pattern of the dependent seeker who is relying on the other to do the work:

> *The more you experience your teacher or the school as giving you what you want, nourishing you, telling you what you need to know, the more you get into that dependent position. The more the teacher doesn't push you to be independent, the more you identify with that positive object relation. That's why the perspective that I'm presenting now, of being grown-up, mature, and independent, will challenge that object relation. You might feel, "Do I really have to go out and do it all myself? Why not just be taken care of? Why not just get all the understanding, the nourishment, and the blessing that's available and things will be okay?"* [1]

Identifying with the positive object relation means you are still expecting to be saved by your relationship with that person. You have been using the other, to take care of you, nourish you, bless you, and also, in a sense, expecting the path of enlightenment to be delivered to you. Your connection with your teacher has become the way you soothe yourself. You have refused to become mature and figure out existence for yourself. This pattern can be unconscious to some extent because we hooked into it when we were babies, and were taken care of so lovingly by our mothers or other caregivers. Thus, at an unconscious level, we are still expecting to be soothed and taken care of in our quest for wholeness rather than being open and vulnerable to the dance of change and letting reality reveal itself. Many of us can carry this pattern our whole lives.

My deconstructing reliance on the awakened other

I myself was enchanted with spiritual teachers like J. Krishnamurti, Nisargadatta, Osho, Papaji, Adi Da and Trungpa. When I started out, I had been particularly enchanted with Osho. I thought this connection with such an exceptional being was going to take me home. Looking back, my attraction made sense. Osho was a former philosophy professor, who gave beautiful discourses in the 1970's, integrating Eastern contemplative traditions with Western philosophy and psychology. In Osho's repertoire of over 650 books and thousands of taped discourses, he laid out a number of different meditations, and covered the range of spiritual pathways to enlightenment. So, for me, there was always another meditation to try, another book to read, another discourse to listen to, and on and on it went. And when the whole routine was concluded, I would try again, expecting different results. The danger is that the larger the projection relating to the guru, the more seemingly insurmountable the whole awakening process becomes for most people. I would fall into the story, "I have a wondrous teacher, I could never be like him". This sets up a perpetual double bind. You believe your guru has the answer for you, but is so marvellous and exceptional that you could never exist like that. The result is bewilderment and dependency.

To get unstuck from this sticky place, it was very helpful for me to realize nobody is awakened, or 'only nobodies are awakened', from which a whole deconstruction process ensued. Awakening is not, after all, a personal thing, it is simply tuning into an awakened existence. Awakened beings, no matter how grand they appear, are actually just nobodies: nobodies inviting nobodies to realize they are nobody. To see awakening as the simple realization that there is no separate self here completely demystifies the whole process. It takes the throne away from all gurus. The open secret is that it is available to us all right here, right now. There is no such thing as an inner sanctuary or a privileged few. The invitation is in this moment. No amount of meditation or effort or discipline is necessary to recognize who I already am in this moment. It merely takes a seeing or recognition right here right now. The gateless gate means that the gate is only an illusion of a boundary; in fact no gate actually exists. We think there is a barrier to get past, but in fact no barrier exists. No attainment is necessary. Awakening is already here, it is our own nature.

Being stuck on the spiritual teacher seems to be a common pattern. I had to be open to seeing that a spiritual teacher like Osho could have many shadow issues. It was apparent to me that in the 1970's he had been flowing along in surrender and giving beautiful discourses, but as he became hugely popular in the early 1980's, the grace and radical transformational energy of previous years seemed to be missing. He appeared more attached to his role, along with the eventually infamous Rolls-Royces, fancy robes, and diamond watches. His once flowing discourses now seemed much more like empty words. What happened to his so-called perfect enlightenment? I found others like me who had been overly impressed by Osho at first, but then had to find freedom on their own. In an interview Kirtan, who had worked with Osho for twenty years but then left him behind, shared his realization that he had to rely on his own awareness:

> *I came to know that I was making a mistake by going to somebody, by asking for the way, by sitting at somebody's feet, by waiting for something to happen, or by desiring that realization may happen with the help of effort and spiritual practice... I began to understand that the desire, the effort, the doings and practices, were the actual disturbances of my peace. The seeking was the obstruction to realization.* [2]

There comes a point when we realize that relying on another, or making some sort of effort, is merely an obstruction. The answer is already directly available within, yet somehow we think another person can supply it for us. The question becomes whether that strategy of relying on somebody else to take us there has been effective, over time. We thought we had found a path, but actually we are as lost as ever because we have never seen into our own nature. We never embraced our own path.

In my own journey, freedom remained elusive until I let go of trying to be saved by the other, until I saw that my reliance on the other kept me in a dependent position. I was lost in the familiar 'safety' limitation, waiting for further goodies from my teacher, instead of going forward to the unfamiliar, which offered no promises, no rewards and no safety. I needed to rely on my own awareness and figure out things myself.

The danger lies in our grand effort to make a short cut to non-dual awakening. We can set ourselves up in a desperately hopeless and helpless double bind. We all want the shortcut to awakening, and we want to get there the fastest way possible, so we start asking for techniques and guidance. The problem is that awakening is a seeing and understanding beyond time and causality, but we want to make it predictable and follow a formula. Spiritual teachers often offer us techniques and pathways towards spiritual success. This is a set-up. Only when a person dies to techniques and pathways does there become the possibility of the *what is* of existence showing up. And spiritual success itself is a mirage, as my own story has shown.

But we get caught by our little techniques whether it is our meditation breathing exercises, our self-inquiry techniques, our little non-dual sayings or hanging out with a guru. These techniques may have delivered us into flowing bliss or oneness at one point, but we get trapped because we have been relying on a technique through time and effort to achieve the awakened state of consciousness. So through effort, and the doing of the ego, we are trying to get there. Any state manufactured through time and effort is lost in time. As soon as the effort goes, the state is gone, and sometimes even before that, as the intensity of the results diminishes, much like an addict with a drug of choice. If only awakening were that cheap and did not require the utter surrender of all that we think we are. But we can get confused, and somehow think that a dualistic approach can deliver us into non-dual being.

The first step has to be a surrender of effort, an embracement of *what is*, as everything else follows the first step. Freedom is found in the first step, not the last step. This is where we can get into trouble, as we rely on some teacher, some technique, or some strategy to produce our awakening. We are lazy, in a way, inasmuch as we do not want to bother to come to a place of true understanding ourselves, but are hoping that the other can do the work for us and take us magically home. We need to see that reliance on the other, whether spiritual guru, teacher, friend or lover, to deliver us, is really just a dressed-up form of begging, as it is not through our own awareness and understanding, our own light, that we are attempting our awakening, but through riding on the coattails of somebody else. We are so busy trying to grab awakening or enlightenment that we are willing to make any sort of deal. And of course these strategies, perhaps somewhat successful in the short term, do not deliver in the long run, as our own understanding has not been awakened.

Colin's dilemma
We must be able to see through pursuing a half-baked awakening based on somebody else's awareness. Colin was

like that, a committed and desperate spiritual seeker. He had been on a journey for many years, and had done many meditative practices. He had been one of the early members who worked with Eckhart Tolle and his insightful teachings on the *Power of Now*. Colin had also embraced the 'waking down' process, and had spent the last twenty years, while running a health food store, going to the workshops of many other touring non-dual teachers. In the last few years, with one non-dual teacher in particular, he had experienced some profound moments in which he was able to embrace formless consciousness in the moment. In sitting and meditating with his teacher, he was able to let go of manifest existence and his mind-body altogether, and enjoy eternal consciousness energy in the moment. For him, after years of seeking, this seemed absolutely thrilling, blissful and wonderful. He could feel a thousand suns arising within himself.

The experiences sitting with his teacher were absolutely beautiful for him. But, the problem became that he could only have these experiences in the teacher's presence. It was a form of unity consciousness, a merging with his teacher, where he felt truly delivered, but the rub was they always required the presence of the teacher. He could never experience these tremendous openings into existence on his own.

When he came to see me, this had been been going on for a couple of years, and now he felt frustrated and in the dark night of the soul. The situation had become repetitive and stale, as he compared his situation to that of a drug addict who needed to purchase a hit from his dealer so he could be okay. He felt desperately trapped in a limbo land; something was very stuck in his seeking. The experience was not conducive to wholeness and embracing non-dual being. It felt like a prison to him and he knew that he could not be true to his own nature while hanging onto his teacher's apron strings.

Colin phoned and asked if he could consult with me. I was more than happy to oblige him but realized that he was going to be terribly disappointed with me, as in no way was I going to repeat this energy transmission game as a pretend solution to his dilemma. In fact, what I was going to do was hand the dilemma of his seeking right back to him. On our appointed day, as we sat together, Colin openly shared his ongoing frustration—how he had tried everything and nothing worked. This latest alliance had left him in limbo land, as he could only get the release from the limited self with the actual alive in-person connection of his teacher. He described the situation as "very screwed up". Yet even in his desperation, he wanted my opinion, because he had come across a new book by a teacher out East, and felt maybe this teacher was really the one who could help him.

I couldn't help but sigh, and I said to him, "Rather than coming up with yet another plan, another teacher, why don't you sit with where you actually are right here, right now?" Colin looked over at me in a puzzled way. I was asking him to simply sit in this place that he had been trying to avoid all along, this place of utter futility and exhaustion, of helplessness and hopelessness. In short, I wanted Colin to sit in the very place that he was trying to escape. He was caught in the addictive pattern of seeking comfort away from *what is*, away from just *being*, through this dependence on the other. Facing *what is* had seemed too uncomfortable.

Now I was inviting him to sit in the utterly lost and panicked place of seeker's hell, in which it feels like one has been scrambling forever, but with no way out. It is here in this very desperate place that the typical response is for the seeker to race to get out of the situation as fast as possible. To avoid this terrifying dilemma, we come up with another desperate strategy, another plan, another teacher, another book. And I was asking Colin to do the opposite. I invited him to resist the temptation to run and try to find another way, and to just sit in this very dark realm where nothing is working out, and be one with it. He was to give up his judgments, and just sit in this place.

Colin tentatively agreed and decided to be present in this dark place that had caused him so much panic and unrest before. I presented Colin with the suggestion, "Nothing can be done, and there is no place to go. There is nothing you can do to save yourself. Give up, let go, stop trying." Expanding on my invitation, I said to Colin, "There is nothing that the mind can do. Nothing can be done as there is no answer for the mind. The situation is absolutely hopeless; there is nothing you can do to save yourself."

As Colin heard these words, at first he seemed to panic even more intensely, and then he started to slow down, as if he was actually stopping trying to save himself. A sense of peace swept across him, something he had not felt for months. A smile broke across his face, as he reported that he felt a spacious vastness of energy. It was evident that the vastness of existence was beginning to flow through him simply through his letting go of effort to save himself in the moment.

Looking closely over at Colin, though, I could see he only lasted here in this state for a couple of minutes. His energy had changed again and I could detect a certain fear and desperation. I asked him what was going on, and he said, "I am trying to figure out how I can keep this going." I smiled to myself, and thought, "Mind, mind, mind", because I had been in the same place too. His mind wanted to make this experience the new answer to his dilemma. I invited him to look right here, right now, to see that he was still adopting a strategy to grasp at something: "You are back still seeking some permanent answer." I added, "What if you allow that there is nothing that you can do in this moment, there is nothing to grab onto? You have been seeking your whole life, and now you're screwed, nothing works, and there is no answer? Just let that in, Colin. There is no answer. Stop trying to save yourself as nothing can be done. There is no answer." I sat back and watched his features distort with horror. His mind seemed to be still spinning to try and come up with some formula or answer to hang onto. I repeated to him, "There is no answer."

I could feel Colin's dilemma as his mind started to confront itself in the realization that there was no answer that the mind could produce. But in this intense chaotic moment, with his mind spinning, he suddenly seemed to be able to accept the news. It was as if his mind stopped struggling, and the black, annihilating abyss energy abruptly shifted into a loving black chasm of being.

A smile broke over Colin's face. He realized he could let it all go and was okay in this space, relinquishing his mind's effort to find an answer. Colin told me he could see that he had been seeking and trying to find an answer for a very long time, but now, "There is no answer for my seeking." He rested in serene beingness, laughing at himself and his goal of finding an answer. I let him enjoy the sublimity of the moment. We sat for fifteen minutes in a transcendent silence and then he said to me with a soft smile, "There is nothing more needed, this is it." I laughed and confirmed his insight. Colin had clearly been able to accept my invitation in the session.

It seems that many seekers eventually come to find their backs against the wall as nothing has worked. The only solution is not to move away from this place but rather remain with nothing to be done and nowhere to go. This goes against the often unspoken premise of the addictive mindset, which takes refuge in reaching out for something or somebody to escape the current emotional state. This tendency is most apparent in the awakening process when the frightening emptiness of the abyss and the prospect of oblivion with no sanctuary are faced. Here many people run to another person or strategy. But, as we saw with Colin, if the seeker can stop running, stop 'efforting' and trying to succeed, reality has a chance to present itself. This is the place where Colin and I rested—and the continual invitation that I left with Colin was for him to see that nothing can be done and there is nowhere to go: just be present in this place of utter desperation, and resist the temptation to embark on another plan or ploy to save himself. To see *what is*.

And as we wrapped up the session, I realized that although we had a breakthrough together, it was now Colin's turn to sit in his aloneness, let go of all seeking, be present and see what emerged. Could he sit in this desert place with no answer? Or would he succumb to the temptations as others do, and run very fast to find some technique or someone else to grab onto? In this moment, my invitation to Colin was embraced. The question was whether he could accept the invitation in the next moment as well. Working with me, he had a breakthrough but the true test would be whether he could abide is this new understanding by himself in each moment of his life. In the end, nobody can let go of the cliff for us. We have to do it by ourselves.

If you are still caught in the grip of the other, look at this exercise:

Exercise 9: **Dropping the other**

✵

In this moment you are going to see if you can move beyond relying on the other to deliver your awakening.

Look through your life and observe your pattern of trying to find a positive object relation to depend on:

Start with your mother or caregiver when you were a baby

See how she nourished you, took care of you, blessed you

Notice how you carried this search on from there for a positive other, possibly your father, teacher, coach, mentor, guide, friend, lover or spouse

See how you wanted each one of these people to take care of you, make you feel like you had a home, save you and be someone you could depend on

Notice how fearful you would become if the other threatened to leave or went away

See how you were clinging on to the other for nourishment and protection

Notice that now you have moved on to the path of awakening, and have found a teacher

Let in how you rely on this teacher to take care of you, soothe you, lay out the path and hopefully awaken you

Notice how you project qualities on to the other person, and do not see them in yourself

It is like you see the diamond in the other person's pocket, but do not see the diamond in your own pocket

Let in the hopelessness of this pattern

See how you could look on the positive object relation forever as the answer, and never meet existence head on, and discover your own diamond nature

Make a decision in this moment that you need to sever the dependency, and learn to rely on your own awareness and surrender directly to existence

Feel the energy that becomes available when you now confront existence directly

You experience existence more intensely

You realize nobody can surrender to existence for you

It is up to you

Chapter 13: From Waiting to Direct Awareness and Inquiry

Firstly, you can't get quickly to where you already are.

Tony Parsons, As It Is

It became obvious to me that many seekers get hooked. We have done everything under the sun but still have a subtle waiting problem. We are conditioned to want some special experience, such as Gautama Buddha's liberation under the Bodhi tree, or indeed the experiences of many other well-known spiritual teachers. We are secretly putting a demand and expectation on existence that we want some wonderful experience to deliver us, when existence is always available right now. We are caught in some fantasy. We want that ultimate experience of being lit up like a thousand suns in utter bliss. There is a striking similarity to to the drug addicted person caught in the endless pursuit of the drug high.

A quantum shift only came to me when I stopped waiting in time for some special experience, and instead surrendered to existence with no expectations. I stopped chasing experiences. Freedom from the self is realized not through fireworks and peak experiences of unity cosmic consciousness but through a seeing through or dropping away of the separate self, an event which may even be quietly peaceful or flat. So, when I work with people, I get them to tune into what is right here, right now, rather than working towards some special experience in the future.

Sometimes I work with people who have been waiting for a grand enlightenment experience almost their whole life. Tim was like that. For forty years, Tim had been waiting for some grand event. He had been meditating for forty years in a Buddhist community, searching for an awakening experience. He had been conditioned to think he needed some bone-jarring awakening experience to set himself free. He had heard so many stories of miraculous awakenings, with wondrous experiences, that he had set up a secret demand from existence: "Give me a miraculous awakening experience." This demand for a special enlightenment experience can keep a person begging for eternity. Waiting for something to happen means anticipating a future event. This is hoping to be delivered by the future, but we are here and now with everything available to us—looking to the future will not help. Does one need an experience to see and be who they already are? By doing or having some wondrous experience, can one actually get any closer to one's own nature? To get the ball rolling with Tim, I read him a statement from the end of a book by Tony Parsons:

The problem is that you think something has to happen. You are waiting for something to happen. It is actually happening continuously, and you simply don't see it. I don't have anything that you don't have. The difference is that I am no longer looking for anything. This is it, and that's the end of it. Give up the search for something to happen and fall in love, fall intimately in love with the gift of presence in "what is". Here, right here, is the seat of all that you will ever long for: It is simple and ordinary and magnificent. You see, you are already home. [1]

After reading this quote to Tim, I looked over at him and I could see that the whole seeking journey was deconstructing right in front of him. He was seeing there had never been a place to go. It had all been a mad, wild goose chase just to get back to this moment. The ground underneath the illusion of the journey was falling away, leaving him with this moment, this here and now.

I decided to carry on. "In this moment, can you just give up the whole Tim trying to become awakened project? See that it is impossible. It can't be done. There is nowhere to go, and nothing can be done. It is all available right here, right now, so why don't we check it out?"

Standing in awareness

Tim was in agreement, so I continued. "Now, the great irony is all of this seeking and coming to the end of seeking is just a preparation for the direct path of inquiry, of standing in awareness. You do not need to ride on anyone's coattails but you can encounter existence directly using the direct path." I paused to let my words sink in, and then added, "You need to use your own awareness and higher reasoning to investigate the difference between objects that arise in awareness and awareness itself." Greg Goode has very nicely summarized the direct path:

> *You examine the gross and subtle worlds, as well as the body, senses and mind. You come to see that they are experienced as objects in witnessing awareness and cannot exist apart from witnessing awareness. You then investigate the witness itself and come to see that it is an ever-so-subtle structure superimposed upon awareness. When this is realized, the witness gently and peacefully collapses into awareness itself, which is pure consciousness. Higher reason establishes that pure consciousness is the truth of the world and your experience at every moment, and leaves you unshakably established in this truth.* [2]

Simplifying this, I said to Tim, "So, having given up seeking, we will just stand in awareness. In this moment, can you see that all you are is consciousness? That chair over there is just arising in consciousness. Every object in the world is just arising in consciousness." Tim nodded, so I carried on. "Now can you see that your body is just an object in consciousness, temporarily arising and then fading away?" Tim smiled in agreement. "And now, Tim, we can use our awareness for thoughts. You have no mind *per se*, no discrete entity or object that can be labelled 'mind'—there are just thoughts—but notice only one thought arises at a time. They rise and they fall away, and are only temporary arisings in consciousness."

I let this settle in, and then stated, "So, you are really just the vast consciousness, nothing binds you, and you are free in this moment." With that, Tim seemed pleasantly surprised. He had been on a journey for forty years, and he had never broken free to simply embrace consciousness. Now the opportunity for total freedom was right here, right now, as it has always been.

A seeing beyond understanding

I continued. "Just to be clear, what is being pointed at here is beyond understanding. Intellectual understanding is important, but this is a seeing beyond time, concepts and thoughts." By Tim's bewildered expression, I sensed I was losing him again. I reminded him, "Remember that no knowing we discussed a few minutes ago? Now, in that place, with open eyes, with nothing to do, and nowhere to go, just relax into the moment. Try it!"

Tim sat with his eyes partially open, in no knowing, with nothing to do and nowhere to go. Within a few seconds I could see by the way his eyes were shining that he was fully in the experience. He laughed out loud, and said incredulously,

"This is it." "Yes, Tim, this is it. As I said earlier, it is an open secret, and it is available right here. Nothing needs to be done, it is all right here. It is just a seeing, beyond words and thoughts, a recognition right here right now; this is it. So, now we can have a cup of tea, and a good laugh at all the foolish nonsense we have gone through to get to seeing, when it is all right here, right now." Looking at Tim, I could feel our interconnected beingness in the moment, and by the light and laughter in his eyes, he seemed to be enjoying the hilariousness of the situation as much as I was.

I celebrated Tim's realization by saying, "So, Tim, here you are and now, in this place, you have received the ultimate medicine of realizing your nightmare and problems have been illusory. So, along with this, it is easy to see that no help was necessary as your problems were illusory, and you were actually okay all the way along, you just did not realize it!" Tim was shining in agreement. "So Tim," I said, "this eternal *now* is your home and it is not dependent on anybody else or any experience."

We sat there in relaxed light and love for ten minutes and then I sent him on his way.

I knew this would be our only session as I did not want Tim to grab onto the other, onto anyone, any thing or any system, by using session work with me as his new dependency. As he left, I invited him to sit in this all on his own and take his ultimate medicine of standing in his own awareness, and continually find his own freedom.

You can try standing in your own awareness for yourself in the exercise overleaf.

Exercise 10: Standing in your own awareness

In this moment see if you can figure out the nature of existence by standing in your own awareness. There is no need to refer to past states or anticipate future states.

Examine the physical (gross) world:

Look at a chair, or any physical object, and notice how it arises in your awareness

The chair is experienced as an object in witnessing awareness and cannot exist apart from witnessing awareness

Give the same attention to your body

See that it does not have an independent existence as it is an object in your awareness

Give the same attention to your senses

See how they arise as something in your awareness

See that they have no independent existence

Give the same attention to your thoughts

See that thoughts are a temporary arising in awareness and disperse back into awareness

There is no separate thinker

Take the attention further

Investigate the witness itself

See that the witness is an ever-so-subtle structure superimposed upon awareness

See how the witness collapses into awareness itself

All is pure consciousness

Part 4
Stage Three Recovery: Living with No Self and Dealing with Re-emerging Seeds of Separation

Chapter 14: Unlocking the Mind's Fixations

> *Now we are trying to find truth through intellect, through imitation—which is idolatry. Only when you discard completely, through understanding, the whole structure of the self, can that which is eternal, timeless, immeasurable, come into being,*
>
> J. Krishnamurti, *The First and Last Freedom*

The honeymoon of awakening

Awakening, wholeness, abiding in non-dual being; this has also been known in Western and Eastern spiritual traditions as the 'marriage of the opposites'. This 'marriage' sometimes has a honeymoon period, and for those of us who suffered with addictive and narcissistic mindsets there may be some areas that still call for attention and resolution—some real work may still await us. At first we feel we might never have another problem as we are both immanent in love and transcendent in full emptiness, with a genuine love for all beings. Life may suddenly feel very easy, with nothing to defend against and nothing to hang onto, in a place of love-bliss. It feels like we have come home to a place that we have always been looking for. It can feel absolutely wondrous in the moment as a big sacred 'yes' is declared to existence. Thoughts may come and go but we don't identify with them like we did before—they pass through like clouds across the sky. There once appeared to be a separate, independent self, but now there is only interconnected existence itself. Before, there was a somebody, and now there is nobody who, paradoxically, is everything and everywhere.

This is the time to look more closely at what can happen after the honeymoon.

Awakening of the mind

Now that there has been a movement into awakening and abiding in non-dual being, we may be surprised and confounded to observe that the mind and thoughts will try to re-assert themselves to regain control. The mind's favorite trick is pretending to help. For example, when there has been an awakening into non-dual being, the mind tries to recreate the experience and find a formula upon which to rely, so awakening will always be guaranteed. You may remember Colin, who wanted to grasp and recreate the 'experience' immediately. The mind wants to hold awakening firmly in its grasp, to erect a sanctuary around some mind-invented secrets of awakening to perpetuate the experience. Unfortunately for the mind, there is no method for the mind to go beyond itself, and thus it may revert to running around in an attempt to hang onto one remedy or another—this is the nature of the mind.

Here, the insights of Adyashanti are helpful. He used the metaphor of awakening of the mind, heart and guts to explain what issues can arise after awakening.[1]

If we turn to the mind, we are reminded how in the journey of awakening, we employ mind to embrace the journey but soon realize that it is mind itself that sends us off track. The mind does not embrace the new, but is focused on the old and the known. Pattern recognition is its forte, so we find it grabbing onto the new to make it 'safe' in the context of old patterns and prejudices. Freedom is found beyond mind, but the nature of the mind is to choose and divide existence into fixed compartments, categories and distinctions. The difficulty is the mind's constant state of judgment. "This is good, this is bad, I don't like this, I like that," the mind says.

The key is to embrace choiceless awareness of *what is*.

It becomes clear that, as Tilopa says, the only answer is an ongoing total demolition of the mind:

Cut the root of a tree and the leaves will wither; cut the root of your mind and samsara falls... Whoever clings to mind sees not the truth of what's beyond the mind.[2]

Thinking cannot do the job—nor can the mind embrace the mystery of the unknown, by some method of the known. What is being sought exists beyond mind. So, instead of believing that our minds can continue to deliver us, we become aware of the limitations of mind and are watchful, as we realize no concept, technique or semblance of knowledge shall be our salvation. For the mind, there is no answer. We have to let go of our addiction of always turning to the mind for the answer. And, as with recovery from any addiction, we stay in our awareness one moment at a time, so we do not fall back into the addictive obsessive cycle of trying to capture the mysteries of existence through mind.

In moving beyond awakening mind we move beyond all concepts and knowledge to embrace *what is*. Nothing can be grasped. Any answer is a grasping. We give up as we realize there is nothing to know and nowhere to go. The mind is no longer grasping onto knowledge or concepts for support and this allows emptiness to be given a free run. And, now we stop relying on mind for support.

When the mind's knowledge, techniques, secret motivations or goals are dropped, we see what remains, as expressed in this story from the life of Bodhidharma, the first Zen teacher from 500 C.E. Bodhidharma, when asked by the emperor, "Who is this Bodhidharma standing in front of me?" replied, "No knowing." Everything has been dropped, and Bodhidharma is left in a place of simple, pure innocence and standing in no knowing. He has gone further than Socrates who stated, "I don't know anything," as even the 'I' has been dropped. Bodhidharma rests in the place of "no knowing" and embraces existence. This is a lovely place to be coming from in each moment.

Similar to this no knowing, Adyashanti described awakening as a destruction of what our mind thinks of as our entire world:

> *What is destroyed is our entire world view—all the ways we are conditioned, all of our belief structures, all of the belief structures of humanity, from the present time to the distant past—all of them go into forming this particular world, this consensus that human beings have agreed upon, this viewing of this as true.* (3)

With awakening, all concepts, knowledge, and world views go up in smoke and we are left in the full emptiness with nothing to hang onto. It is a beautiful place of non-conceptual awareness.

Subtle tricks of the mind: dealing with re-emerging seeds of separation

After awakening, we can be in a wondrous place for days, months, seasons, even years. Then it may happen that in a heartbeat we are be yanked back into our separate selves, as if we are at the end of a bungee cord that extended into the abyss and is now contracting, bouncing back up into our past issues, emotional wounds and overlooked patterns. It may not be so dramatic for some—a person may have been quite well integrated with few issues 'before'. But in any event, out of mystical celebration, we can be returned to the grit of contraction, wounds and separation. And sadly, we believed that with awakening, the healing work was behind us. We now see there is more work to come as all of our neglected, uncooked seeds of issues wildly sprout into awareness with the energy upgrade of awakening. And perhaps for those of us who have been caught up in the false freedoms of addiction and narcissism there will be a swift and sure recognition of those seeds. We will recognize that the after-awakening work is upon us.

Firstly, we can recognize our addictive tendencies in that we want to have an awakening, and have it all behind us—it's a new slant on the immediate gratification we have sought for so long. We want one final vast transcendence experience and be done forever. But life comes in the present, so we have to learn to deal with what life delivers us in each moment. The key here is to be open to anything that arises, and not assume that all the issues are behind us because of awakening.

The mind can be a very cunning trickster as it loves to co-opt things for itself. Even after awakening to our real nature, the mind can come through the back door, grab concepts and fixate on labels. A common pattern is for the mind to attach to transcendence, but this is just another way to fixate and cling to a particular point of view.

Clinging to nothingness: witnessing and false detachment

This hanging out in transcendence can be combined with a fixation of hiding out in the witness position. We can get stuck in the detached witness position and feel we are free of the 'me'. The key here is to see the elements of ego that are hiding in the witnessing position to avoid a full embracement of life. This avoidance has a parallel in the way we used our addiction to avoid life, too. It is a remarkable realization to come across the subtle separate 'I' in the witness position. People have told me, or we have discovered in therapy sessions, that it seems to be so subtle that they cannot see it. But if a person clearly turns within, using inquiry, and asks,

"Who is witnessing the witness?" or, "Who is transcending?" an awareness comes to light. One literally can see the 'I' thought buried within this so-called detached witness. In seeing it, the "I" thought crashes back to the source.

Similar to the issue of identifying with the detached witness is the problem of identifying with nothingness. A person does not realize that an attachment to nothingness has developed through making this nothingness the new object. In fact, identifying with a detached nothingness can cause a drastic split in day-to-day life. There is an "I" thought identifying with nothingness. As former seeker, Jeff Foster, realized, detachment and identification with the void was in its own way a dualistic retreat from everyday reality. This realization allowed him to be released back into intimacy with life:

> *I abided in emptiness, but there was still a 'me' doing the abiding. The emptiness had not yet collapsed into fullness. I hadn't died yet... Finally, the detachment collapsed. Everything does eventually. Finally, there was the death of the person, the person who could be detached or not, and a revelation, for no-one, that this is it. The joylessnesss fell away, and there was a plunge into the absolute mystery of it all... totally beyond words, totally beyond language.* [4]

Foster's collapse allowed him to return to intimacy with existence. Just as the Heart Sutra states, "Form is emptiness and the very emptiness is form; emptiness does not differ from form, form does not differ from emptiness; whatever is form, that is emptiness, whatever is emptiness, that is form." [5] We can have intimacy with form, as it is the emptiness itself.

This pattern of grasping onto a transcendent nothingness witnessing position and becoming a detached observer of life is very common. In my own personal experience and also in working as a non-dual psychotherapist, I have found that the only remedy is to, firstly, observe the calamity of this position and, secondly, embrace the absolute failurehood of it. Working this through can usher in an experience of deconstruction and a crashing of the fixed position, resulting in a collapse back into the intimacy of life. In the following case study, we examine how this can fully unfold.

Paul's collapse

People who have had an awakening can get stuck in the void, attached to this state, possessing a sense of superiority about it all. They then reluctantly arrive at therapy realizing at a deep level that this position is not working. Paul, in his early thirties, was this type of person. When he came for therapy, he was detached and uninvolved in his relationships. His girlfriend was about to leave him. His work relationships were also typically sour. Paul worked as a counselor and found that, over the last few years, he experienced a repeating cycle of preliminary excitement when he started to work with a new counseling agency, then quickly thereafter the agency began to distance itself from him, and later would not renew his contract. He found this strange as he felt he had embraced the teachings of loving kindness, and yet, in his superior aloofness, he was in fact closed off from life. Paul's understanding, however, was that he was being betrayed by life.

Paul's girlfriend had asked him to attend a counseling session or two with me. So here he was. He came into the office with an air of nonchalant superiority. When I asked Paul how it was going, he relished telling me stories of encountering people and spinning them with his superior stance. I could see the problem. He was attached to his non-dual state. In each moment, even the personalization of awakening has to be let go of. In the stillness of this moment, there is no concept of enlightenment or awakening, just the mystery of existence.

There are no formulas to follow. The mind loves to co-opt things and hang out in non-dual land, after the 'honeymoon'. Tragically, through the use of non-dual formulas and clichés, there can be a withdrawal from facing and loving *what is* in each moment. There are no concepts more slippery than the concepts of awakening and being in the void. Paul was fixated in his detached nothingness and his idea of himself being an awakened being.

Life usually gives us our transformational opportunity and one was given to Paul. After recounting all of his recent non-dual encounters, he got to the concrete problem. Not only had he just gone through a round of counselor job applications, with no job offers at all, but he was even laid off from the current job he had. Behind his nonchalant and superior air, Paul was devastated and looking for answers. In the counseling session, we tried examining his pattern to see what the world was mirroring back to him. "You know what is real and others don't," I said to him. He knew he was better than everyone because of the "non-dual" place he had reached in his journey; "The other fools don't know what is going on", was his attitude.

To help crack open Paul's heart, I had to confront him with the total failurehood of his stance. I could see plainly that Paul had made the void an object to be grasped. Paul had to learn to let go of his fixed position of attachment to the void and his superior nonchalance—it was almost an attachment to non-attachment. I invited him to see that this was the same old game of narcissism set up in a new fancy way. It was his chance to feel superior to the other. I pointed out to him, "You have become attached to the void, and that has become your new identity. You feel that you are this awakened person coming from the absolute. This is narcissism, thinking you are this awakened guy hanging out in the void."

My initial invitation did not seem to stick with Paul so I

followed up with a pointer. I invited Paul to realize there was only this beingness, this life, this now, *only this*. It all comes down to embracing *this*. In the intensity of *this*, all is revealed.

Paul and I then meditated on the 'isness' of the moment with nothing to hang onto. As we sat there in the translucent light, it became obvious, in a very ordinary way, that all of existence was illuminated and enlightened. There was nothing special to grasp, and no claim to be made. As he turned inward, Paul could clearly see the 'I' thought hanging on to emptiness and the idea of non-dual being. His sense of superiority was swept away in a heartbeat. Suddenly, he crashed back down to just *this*. As his heart broke wide open, his beingness was hurled against the rocks of existence. He could see clearly that there is nothing to hang onto. The bottom had dropped out and he could no longer hang onto his superior position. He was interconnected and ordinary all at once.

As we sat there embracing the mystery of this, I could feel the concepts of awakening and enlightenment disappearing from Paul. He was ordinary again in a total acceptance of existence. There was no more a distinction to be made between self and others. With a smile, Paul explained that he could see that he no longer needed to *try* to practice loving kindness. Realizing the utter failurehood of his superior stance had blown his heart wide open and now he felt much more intimate with existence and free to love —the idea of 'efforting' to love was discarded without a second thought. We left our session work there, with my invitation to Paul to keep blown wide open with nothing to hang onto in each moment.

Before we continue to the next chapter, about the awakening of the heart, you can check out your own no knowing awareness for yourself with the exercise on the following page.

Exercise 11: Embracing no knowing

※

See if in this moment you can accept the limitations of mind, as, in awakening, the mind does not have the answer to how to become awakened.

> Allow yourself to come from a place of no knowing:
>
> *Realize that no concept, technique or semblance of knowledge is the answer*
>
> There is no construct to hang onto
>
> Embrace the simplicity of no knowing
>
> *See that there is nothing to hang onto in this moment*
>
> Relax into being
>
> *See and feel the innocence of no knowing energy in the moment*
>
> In this moment, enjoy the utter relaxation of not knowing anything
>
> *Experience how still, relaxing and translucent this is*
>
> *In no knowing you are connected to the vast consciousness of existence*

Chapter 15: The Unfinished Business of the Heart

The attempt to avoid facing the unresolved issues of the conditioned personality only keeps us caught in their grip.

John Welwood, *Toward a Psychology of Awakening*

The awakening of the heart involves an opening up to all things and beings, so that we become a loving presence interconnected with existence. Typically, we would have loved one apparently separate person exclusively, or have confined our love to the immediate circle of people we call 'ours'. Now there is a movement away from those typical affairs of the heart, where we were limited and object-focused, to an expansive and inclusive appreciation of all. With this opening up of love, we move beyond the confines of lust and romantic love to become friendly with all of existence. We become non-possessive, with no jealousy and no desire to dominate, as we acknowledge the unconditional freedom of the other.

We can begin to enjoy the simple things of existence, where once we craved the extra stimulation of our addiction or acknowledgement of our specialness. Now there is delight as our natural state. Here, compassion and action do not spring from 'shoulds' and 'oughts', but are spontaneous expressions of our nature. We live in gratitude, embracing the many gifts of existence with no demand at all.

Spiritual bypass: escaping our dark emotions

Working with the heart, however, can reveal a whole new set of unresolved matters that might surprise us, because we take refuge in avoidance, rather than indulging our craving for stimulation. In her book on healing the dark emotions, Miriam Greenspan observed that humans tend to avoid and escape dark emotions such as grief, fear and despair with a range of avoidance strategies.[1] A favorite one is that, in our attempts at spiritual transcendence, we use spiritual practice to do what we call 'rising above' our emotional and personal issues—all those messy, unresolved matters that have the potential, we feel, to weigh us down. Transpersonal psychologist, John Welwood, has called this tendency "spiritual bypass". We sweep the dust and debris of our unresolved issues under the carpet of our new spiritual identity.[2]

Everything can show up once again, even after awakening. Feelings can be more acute than ever as now we are an open door to existence. Hate, envy, jealousy, greed, fear, shame are all invitations to look at the illusion of separation that is arising in the moment. The most negative emotions can be tracked to anger, fear and judgment, which stem from believing our thoughts—or even believing that we *are* our thoughts. This means we are perceiving from a state of division, not from wholeness. Adyashanti urges us to unpack all of this:

> *As soon as one feels emotional conflict, the questions that should be asked are: In what way am I going into division? At this moment, what's causing this sense of separation, isolation, or protectiveness? What is it that I'm believing? What assumptions have I made that are being reproduced in my body and made manifest as emotion?* [3]

We can have all sorts of uncooked seeds to deal with related to some deep assumptions around our sense of separation and clinging back to our separate 'I'.

Myself, I had to work initially on occasional patterns of grasping at my university professorship, in which I switched from a loving presence to clutching and attachment to the university gig. I looked at the stories I was creating and could see that the only release from this was to let go of the 'I' that I was hanging onto in the moment. This was actually easy as the clinging 'I' was just a thought. I would ask, "Who is feeling fear?" When I looked within, I would come across a clinging 'I' thought and, in an intense moment of awareness, I would see the 'I' thought dissolve back into nothingness and consciousness. Freedom in a heartbeat! All by looking intensely within. When the 'I' thought is let go of, the fear just dissolves back into energy too. It all becomes 'not-two' once again in the moment. Rather than going to the past to work out some method or antidote, freedom came just by turning within very intensely, seeing the hidden 'I' thought and letting it dissolve in awareness.

Some of us may have more emotional residue to work through than others. We will now consider a recent case involving a person who had a very sudden awakening experience and the leftover injustice stories that he needed to deal with.

Ross's rage around injustice

Ross had a sudden awakening experience in his mid 40's when he suddenly lost his sense of being a separate self. After a month of sublime enjoyment, a report was made to university security regarding Ross's odd behavior related to him driving slowly and watching deer dance in the sprinklers at night. He was called in for a security investigation. Despite the fact that the investigation went no further, the intense, institutional, police-style questioning plunged him into the anger and the sense of injustice and betrayal that he had been carrying his whole life. As he drove home after the interview, he found himself tormented and angry, his blissfulness gone. This recent injustice reminded him of many other injustices in his life.

He came to my office the next day, and together we worked on seeing this recent event as a transformational opportunity. I pointed out to him that he was still carrying a lot of old stories about injustice and betrayal, and that he needed to burn through them. He had been inadvertently looking for this non-dual place his whole life as he had never fitted in—he had always felt like an outsider. But now I could see Ross still had some old tapes to burn through, and we agreed he would commence work on the sense of injustice and betrayal that he had been carrying since a child. I suggested this incident could be a catalyst for him to re-author his life according to his non-dual awakening. Ross said he wanted to do this re-authoring in conjunction with Byron Katie's work on the four questions, to facilitate burning through his stories.[4]

When I followed up with him a week later, Ross said he was now in the middle of the process of what Jed McKenna called spiritual autolysis.[5] This is a journal writing process to let go all that is false. Ross could see that he had a whole variety of stories, some creepy crawlers, some big trees and some little trees. From a place of no self, he was able to let go of these stories and realize that freedom was found in the perfection of each moment. His recent incident of injustice led to him to discover that there were about seven or eight other incidents that he was still carrying around. Ross was able to let these stories go, seeing them as false, and he became light and ecstatic once again.

As Ross resolved his stories of injustice, other intense emotions emerged. For instance, he found himself revisiting his fear. He had made some professional counseling commitments before his awakening, and now he could see many of those commitments were made with the motivation of being validated by an agency. Now in his free-flowing state, he could feel himself falling into the fear of having to manage those commitments. He wanted, in this moment, to make the future, in this case the facilitation of a counseling group next week, totally secure. He also wanted to guarantee his good rapport with the agency. This was a re-assertion of an old addictive pattern of grabbing at a future moment trying to make it secure in this moment, which of course is impossible and only magnifies the fear. Even in this moment it is impossible to make the separate self secure, let alone to do so in a spurious, non-existent future. This becomes evident with self-inquiry if we look closely into who is feeling this fear. With awareness, the sense of the apparent separate self dissolves back into the source. [6]

As we worked on this issue, I asked Ross if he could see how he was grabbing at the self in a future moment in an attempt to make next week secure. Furthermore, his pattern of begging for validation from the agency counselors was also causing him to feel that the flow of wholeness was being disrupted. I presented him with the challenge, "Can you see that you are begging for self-other validation, and trying to make the future moment secure? The self, the 'I' thought, is trying to grab at some secure place and this is psychologically impossible. Can you see the prison you are creating for yourself, and let it all go once again right here, right now?" With this, Ross smiled, and he told me, "Yes, I can let it all go," and he laughed. He laughed because he could see immediately that the knot in his stomach was gone—the fear and the limitation were gone. Away he went, realizing that this work would be an ongoing process. Ross had worked on his judgments and stories of injustice, and now he had revisited fear. And he understood there was more to come. Ross was just embarking on the path of learning to live from non-dual being. Like Ross, we all need to keep looking at our unfinished emotional issues and see where we might have tried to bypass issues by being 'spiritual'.

Exercise 12: **Working through unresolved emotional issues**

✻

Identify in this moment if there is an unresolved issue you need to work on.

> Face your issue directly:
>
> If there is some left-over pain, trauma, feeling, resentment, experience it directly
>
> Sit in the unresolved issue, let all the pain and feelings in
>
> Look closely at what is arising
>
> *In the moment, see the clutching at an apparent separate self 'I' in the midst of what is arising*
>
> Notice that the more you look directly for the 'I' the more it dissolves by itself
>
> *Feel the freedom of seeing there is no actual separate self 'I' here, it was just an assumption*
>
> Notice that with the dissolving of the 'I' your judgment of the situation drops
>
> *See how easily you move into choiceless awareness of your emotions*
>
> Notice that the emotions dissolve by themselves in awareness
>
> *The emotions are only temporary arisings*
>
> *You are free just by dissolving the separate self 'I' in the moment*

Chapter 16: Grasping at Survival in the Guts

The fear of no-self is the mother of all fears, the one upon which all others are based.

Jed McKenna, *Spiritual Enlightenment: The Damnedest Thing*

We can understand awakening in the mind as embracing no knowing, spaciousness and transcendence, and awakening in the heart as freeing the heart up for an overflowing of love and connection to all that exists, sometimes known as the 'ten thousand things'. But it is in the guts where things get really interesting. A person can have tremendous awakening experiences but still face problems around the issue of no-self. In the guts, we feel our primal need to survive, as we face no-self and nonexistence—the abyss that we have looked at earlier. Becoming aware of our primal grasping at survival, we can experience desperation and panic as the fear of no-self overwhelms us. Increasingly aware of consciousness opening up in our bellies, we can feel the vastness of existence, a terrifying impersonality and the reality of the sense of perceived self-annihilation. In the fear of not existing in the moment we may desperately grab onto some sense of self in the knot of our belly as we defend against the abyss of no-selfhood.

Here, the primal fear of the annihilation and extinction of the self is revealed in all of its gut-wrenching intensity. This is where reality bites. It can be absolutely shocking to a person when the terror of no-self suddenly flashes through them, sometimes very unexpectedly as the so-called 'self' thrashes wildly in the abyss trying to find something to attach itself to. Even in our deepest addictions, we can be unconsciously trying to find oblivion and escape the misery of the egoic self. Yet, when we fall into the no-self state either unconsciously through drugs or consciously in the middle of a meditation retreat, the terror of no-self makes us want to run. It only takes an instant for the illusory self to crumble, sometimes leaving us very shocked. For instance, Suzanne Segal wrote about how she stepped on to a transit bus, and suddenly in a heartbeat her normal self disappeared, and all that was left was no-self. [1] She spent ten years seeking help from traditional therapists. Eventually she started working with non-dual teachers who mirrored to her the non-dual transformation potential of this movement in her. Relief only came when she stopped judging the experience and learned just to accept it. What is clear, as evidenced by Suzanne's story, is that a primal terror can erupt inside when the self has fallen away. A person can make the mistake of desperately trying to grab at a sense of self instead of moving towards wholeness by being at one with the abyss.

In my own journey, it was only in sitting in the black energy space of non-existence without judgment that I could see that there was no self, and at the same time there was a sense of presence. This presence was felt in a darkness that revealed itself to be a brilliant translucent light. Similarly, Jeff Foster pointed to the great death that arises through simply seeing that no one is there; in the absence of self there is an extraordinary fullness:

You have to lose your life to save it. And so when there is no-one, there isn't an empty void, a lonely and joyless black space devoid of all qualities, no, no, no. That void is full, it is bursting with life. With the sea roaring, and seagulls screeching, and the wind crashing against your face, and a steaming cup of tea, and.... life, damn it life! The emptiness is fullness, the void is fully alive, the nothingness is life in all its magnificence, and that is the freedom that the so-called 'individual' could never, ever find. (2)

What is amazing is that in the whole journey we assume there is a problem. When a person tunes into existence, it becomes obvious this is an incorrect assumption. There is no person, just the vastness of existence. Nobody was there in the first place as something separate and cut off from existence itself. Freedom was already here, all the way along.

We now turn to consider a case study that illustrates the benefit of a seeing that there is nobody here in each moment, and that there can be a non-judgmental resting in presence.

Tom's fearful folding before his non-dual presentation

A person can enjoy the freedom of many experiences when abiding in non-dual beingness and yet, at the same time, still have many uncooked seeds which give life to a separate self. At a subtle level, there can be seeds of internalized self-other object relations. In my experience, lecturing on transpersonal psychology and non-dual being has its own special transformational opportunity. A person can feel they are flowing along in non-dual beingness, but when presented with the opportunity of publicly speaking about non-dual being, uncooked seeds may emerge as an inadvertent demand to be appreciated or to be understood. I have seen clearly that I need to be prepared to die in the moment. If I don't accumulate anything, including letting go of any need for creating a good impression or favorable reception, I am ready to die in each moment as I have nothing to lose. There is nothing to cling to, no knowing and no self, and I am free to embrace the isness of the moment.

We have already noticed that the mind can be tricky. When preparing for a lecture or talk, the mind can start grasping at security. In this moment the mind demands a guarantee that the lecture a few days away will be totally successful. J. Krishnamurti spent a lifetime teaching the wisdom of insecurity, in that there is no such thing as psychological security. He said, "Where ever there is a desire for self-protection, there is fear. When I see the fallacy of demanding security I do not accumulate anymore." The paradox is that, "Whatever the mind does to get rid of fear causes fear."[3] The strategies that we act upon to fend off fear actually create fear. The more we try to be secure, the more fearful we become. So, like Jiddu Krishnamurti, I have seen the fallacy in demanding security for a future moment. I have found I have to surrender all, die to the moment, and let it all go. This is not a one shot deal but instead needs to be re-visited time and time again.

An associate of mine, Tom, was preparing for a presentation on non-dual transformation. A few weeks earlier he phoned me to discuss his intentions. Over the last ten years, Tom had had many ground-breaking non-dual experiences, and even in the last year had moved into spending increasing amounts of time in a place of extraordinary absence of self. During our telephone conversation, I told him to be prepared to let it all go; in speaking of the non-dual it becomes clear there is no sanctuary to be found anywhere. He did not entirely grasp my meaning, interpreting my words to mean that perhaps he could let go of all the presentation materials that he had prepared.

Tom came to see me on the day of his presentation. He had not slept the previous night. Instead, he had lain in bed with his mind spinning fiercely. Fear had shown up in a sudden and profound way and he found himself grasping at a sense of self and security. In the moment, he wanted a guarantee that his presentation would go well, be positively received and culminate in an appreciative acceptance by his peers. As he frantically scrambled for some security in the moment, he found that there was nothing available to grasp onto. He had spent the whole night spinning, with intense energy racing through him. Tom was shocked by this sleepless night, as he had had an experience of no-self the previous summer, and believed he existed in that place on a regular basis since that time. And now, his mind was spinning, almost out of control.

It was clear to me that even though Tom was coming from a place of mostly abiding in non-dual being, there was a subtle seed in him whereby he had the desire to give an impressive talk and be appreciated by others. Tom, in his own way, was still demanding and hoping for mirroring back from the appreciative other. In short, he had not fully let go of his desire to make a good impression. Since the presentation subject was about non-duality, the stakes were even higher, as Tom would be interacting with non-dual colleagues with whom he already had established relationships. That old codependent addictive pattern of trying to create security through taking care of others was re-emerging. As Jiddu Krishnamurti might have said, Tom was caught in the illusion that he could create psychological security, and his mind was churning over in a desperate bid for that elusive sense of security.

When Tom came to see me for that emergency session on the day of his presentation, he was experiencing a heightened state of panic. He felt that he had a monkey mind grasping desperately for some semblance of security. He sat down and announced, "I am folding... I can't pull this talk off today." I looked over at Tom and invited him consciously to accept the negative, panic-stricken feelings rather than resist them.

I asked, "Can you accept there is no answer for the mind and let the ego-self die right here, right now?" To die consciously in the moment was his task and to let go of his desires for appreciation and the 'need' to have his wisdom and specialness recognized by others.

I could see Tom was frightened and struggling within, but soon he stopped trying to save himself. He sat there and allowed himself to die in the moment. A sudden deep calm and vast flowing presence washed through him. He was no longer clinging to a separate, special self. He said, "I've let it all go, I am okay, I can do this presentation." He sat there relaxed, feeling fearless, when just a few minutes earlier he had been overwhelmed by anxiety. I left him alone in my office in his let-go state so Tom could just be with the stillness of dying to all of the demands of impressing others. Fifteen minutes later he met me in the hall, smiling serenely, and said, "I'm ready to go." And as he walked toward the nearby presentation room, I could see he was in an accepting place, with no self to grab onto and protect. His task of awareness would be to remain in this place of no-self during his talk.

After his presentation, Tom reported that he was able to stay in this place for most of his talk, except for a few moments of mind spinning and grabbing in response to a difficult question. However, he was able to let go quickly and abide in the present moment. Overall, Tom had found this whole 'dying to his talk' experience to be an excellent transformational opportunity.

Perhaps, we all secretly hope that the fire of awakening will burn through all of our issues. We want to celebrate an awakening which does not require us to keep working on our issues. For many of us, though, this is not the case and we have much more to process, as there remains the tendency to be pulled back into patterns of the separate self. Each moment affords us a new invitation to surrender and work through the fixated mind pattern, or the judgmental feeling; an invitation to come back to embracing no-selfhood in our guts, fully participating in the mystery of an embodied life. Rather than hiding our issues under the concept of 'awakening', we can accept the invitation to realize that there is nobody here, and to be free in our mind, heart and guts.

An intense issue, as we have seen in this chapter, is grasping at survival. Check out your own fear of no-self in the following awareness exercise.

Exercise 13: Fear of no-self and not surviving

❋

In this moment, whether you have had many awakening experiences or a few 'glimpses', see that there still may be a fear of no-self deep in your being. At the deepest level, the fear of not surviving shows up as a felt sense in our belly. Our most primal existential grasping at survival is stored in our guts.

> Think of a situation which threatens your survival:
>
> Place your awareness into your inner belly.
>
> Be with whatever you experience in your belly without judgment
>
> *Have no opinion as to what arises*
>
> Even if it feels like numbness or nothing, be with that.
>
> *Just be okay with what is*
>
> Now, look for a subtle tension or grasping in your belly
>
> *It is the separate self 'I' contracting*
>
> *It can feel almost like a claw, or a closed fist*
>
> Notice how it has always been here, just sometimes you were not aware of it
>
> *See if you can feel the primal grasping for survival*
>
> Notice how desperate this grasping is
>
> *See if you can feel how easily it increases into a panic state*
>
> Notice all of the ways you try to manage or escape this grasping at surviving
>
> *Realize nothing ever works*

Notice how you always return to this grasping and fear place

See nothing works, the fear of no-self is always there

See how this perpetual fear and grasping could go on forever

Feel how doomed this is

Recognize how futile this is

See that this grasping could put you in unending misery

See that you have no choice but to let go

Release your grasp on surviving

Give up, let go of the separate self 'I'

Don't hang onto anything

Just be in the vastness

See that you are one with existence

There is no self there, but everything is okay

You have let go of the 'I'

There is just existence

You are the vastness itself

Just be the vastness

Part 5
Abiding in Non-dual Being in Daily Life

Chapter 17: The Hollow Bamboo: Letting Go of Personal Will

Like a hollow bamboo rest at ease with your body.

Tilopa, *Song of Mahamudra*

Letting go of personal will

For a long time I was propelled by private goals and was using my so-called personal will. The use of personal will seemed to be so much a part of my immersion in the American Dream. I was using determination and effort to achieve success, to achieve my goals. I had mistakenly thought that my personal will, all under the control of that very special 'me', could take me all the way to success, even when I moved onto the path of awakening. The result of all of this addiction to the separate self was, of course, failure and exhaustion. But as I let go of the separate self, and dissolve into the ocean of existence, I am no longer propelled by a personal, self-regarding and very limited will, but by a spontaneous, joyful and compassionate wholeness. It was always a struggle working with that personal will, because I was almost striving against existence itself. It was like a small wave trying to change the direction of the whole ocean, always trying to go in its own direction, and not recognizing that it is part of the whole and that it needs to relax and be taken by the ocean—the ocean from which the wave is not separate.

So, rather than perpetuate the suffering of identification

with my personal will and battle against the whole of existence, I allow myself to be part of the ocean, existence and being. Now I can sing the song of existence, which is no longer a private song, but the song that is created as existence passes through. I am enjoying what Tilopa called being the 'hollow bamboo'. Like a hollow bamboo I offer no resistance as existence sweeps through me—I cling to nothing.

Existence flows through me in day to day life. The energy of existence pours through and I am like a conduit in which there is no self.

The Buddha talked about just being a log and floating down the river, soon to be merged with the ocean. Whether one is a hollow bamboo or a log, what is entailed is surrender and giving up—floating with existence. This is what the old cliché 'going with the flow' points to. When the log gets caught on something, we can just check to see if there is grasping going on of one sort or another or trying to survive. Are we trying to protect our separate self-existence? Similarly, when the passageway of the hollow bamboo is blocked, we can just look inwardly and let go of inner clutching and grabbing on. Soon, once again, existence is dancing through us.

Something happens as we get out of the way and let life flow through us. We simply efface ourselves completely. There is a simple formula for this: we just have to let the sense of our separate self die. It is as if we can only be devoted to one master; but when we are simply trying to live and survive no matter what, our separate self has not died yet, and has not been resurrected into true existence beyond our own death. By dying to our separate selves, we no longer have to be in contention or competition with the rest of existence; we have accepted existence and died in our own death, so all of existence is friendly now, and nobody is our enemy. Thus, we do not have to utilize myriad strategies to establish and protect ourselves. We are open to working with all of existence, and see all beings as enlightened—some just have not realized it yet. As we pour our message out, we are grateful if it is received in any way; being a ripe fruit it is truly a gift to be picked and eaten. It is wonderful to be overflowing with energy and share it with whoever is ready to receive the gift of energy and love.

Existence becomes a play, not a serious endeavor. Letting existence flow through us like a hollow bamboo allows us to share our energy in the cosmic play of existence and it is no longer a grave and portentous matter. There have been so many awakened people before us, and there will be even more after us, so we can delight in sharing the insights of people who once walked the earth, as there is such a rich legacy of awakened teachings from which we can draw. In the moment, we can be hollow bamboos, let their energy sweep through us, and we become conduits for their message. In a way the song remains the same, and in a way the song in this moment is always new and fresh. People have been awakening for thousands of years, and have left their tracks for us to see. We can follow their tracks and learn from them, and at the same time, always know that we must become a light unto ourselves. Awakening has to become our own understanding.

The song of awakening is changing, although how can awakening itself change? Here in the twenty-first century we seem to be more savvy but also more gullible, more well-informed and yet more ignorant. There is an information overload, so that we become almost numb as we try to untangle all the different perspectives and dogmas which call out for our attention.

Awakening can no longer be an escape from life. We have to be willing to live life all the way up, to cherish all of our connection, and our day to day life as something to be honored and not run away from. We can bring our awakening into our institutions and our educational systems, so life as we know it is transformed. No longer are we limited by our narrow ego-absorbed view, so there is no way we can afford to be aloof to the demands of saving this great planet from destruction. Thus, it is not so much awakening *from* life, but awakening *to* life. We can bring our awakened state to the dream that we call our ordinary life, so that it is an extraordinarily blessed existence. *Samsara* and *nirvana* become one.

So, the song of awakening is a song of awakening into this life. We can participate intensely, all the time at ease with all, because we have already let it all go. We have already made our home in the vastness of existence. The gift of life is something to be truly honored and cherished. In awakening we can share the love of *what is* with those around us. We can invite people to a place beyond the misery of separate self and the cut-off isolation of ego and suffering to an embracement of *what is*. So, we can become hollow bamboos in the middle of ordinary life.

In my work with people, whether it is my non-dual group workshops, private practice or teaching university addictions counseling students, each moment is the opportunity to let existence flow through and put out the invitation to others to embrace the open secret that it is all right here right now in this moment. The message flows through the hollow bamboo; this is it. Try it for yourself.

Exercise 14: Embracing the hollow bamboo

*

In this moment you are going to free yourself so the energy of existence can flow through you by being a hollow bamboo.

> Imagine yourself a hollow bamboo:
>
> You are hollow inside, with nothing to hang onto
>
> *You have no self, no thoughts, no feelings, no problems*
>
> Now feel existence just flowing right through you
>
> *The energy will flow right through the hollow bamboo of your whole being*
>
> Notice any areas of holding or tension in your body and just let it go
>
> *See how the energy washes away any pain or woundedness*
>
> Delight in the energy of existence flowing through you
>
> *You are a conduit for existence*
>
> *The dance of existence flows through you*
>
> *Healing happens by just being a hollow bamboo*

Chapter 18: Touch and Let Go in Relationships

My experience is that I need no one to complete me. As soon as I realize that, everyone completes me.

Byron Katie, *I Need Your Love – Is that True?*

Touch and let go

In the intensity of awakening, we look around at existence and see there is no permanent entity there, either with self or with the other. Everything is impermanent and exists through relativity and relationship. We can see that so much of our previous seeking was about trying to grab some sense of permanent self. This grabbing is at the heart of addiction, as we clutch at substances, people and behaviors to reaffirm our sense of a separate special self. But as we awaken, we awaken out of the dream of separate self-existence, and we enjoy the vast interconnectedness and suchness of existence. As we take this awakening into day to day life, we have to watch for any back-door grabbing, as we need to stay in a let-go place. Nothing can be hung onto.

The secret of Zen has been described as "Touch and let go". [1] This means being able to enjoy the moment of connection in our relationships, jobs and life in general—but not to hang on. True renunciation is being able to let all attachments go in each moment, without clutching onto anything. It is embracing the wisdom of insecurity, and being vulnerable in this moment. When asked what his secret was, the Buddha just showed an open hand to the inquirer. I allow myself to be exactly in the place that in my own way I had tried to avoid for so long—vulnerable insecurity with nothing to hang onto. Just being in this full emptiness with none of the grasping or the props that the ego loves to hang onto.

This does not mean staying away from relationships. I can completely enjoy an intimate relationship, but I realize that in each moment the whole relationship can be enjoyed, and then let go. I look over and see this beautiful heartfelt being who happens to be my wife and feel our love intensely connecting in this moment. I look over with love at this wondrous creature who is my wife. I am shocked by the eternal dark beauty shimmering through her, but she is not mine to possess or grasp onto. I can't assume it will go on and on. Life is dangerous and human love is precious and vulnerable; it does not have the stable enduring power of a rock, but the vulnerable delicacy of a rose whose petals have opened. I am free to enjoy and savour this moment, but we are not talking about a conscious letting go in each moment. It's more just *being* with no need to hang on or to let go. We come to a place where we have let go even of letting go.

When love is intense, death is there as well. There may be an intensity beyond self or other, as all walls are collapsed and two beings enjoy total interconnectedness. The touch of love is wonderfully sacred and beautiful, but can't be nailed down or made secure. It is a case of touch and let go. So, rather than grabbing for love, I can embrace the beingness of love in each moment without making demands on the other. So many people I have worked with are worried that if they come from a place of vulnerable love in the moment, they will be wounded and hurt. But that means their love and vulnerability has conditions and expectations tied to it—remnants of the separate self ego—that create misery and are better dropped.

In coming from a place of love, there is no room for the petty tyrant demands of the ego. We die into love. And we fall in love with all of existence, our love has become an interconnected love for all beings and aspects of existence. The only real barrier will be if we hang onto ourselves as separate and special. By allowing the death of the self, we can be reborn into love. Thus, the invitation becomes to abide in love, without all of the foolish and miserly demands of the self. Love is no longer a contractual business deal based upon what a person can get out of it. but an overflowing presence of love in the moment that has dropped all demands on the world. "Love conquers all for those who are conquered by love." [2]

Intermingling of love and the 'killer'

As well as the ability to touch and let go, awakening into non-dual being seemed to change another long-term pattern in me, as I began to notice a heartfelt ability to lay things on the line in the moment. Previously, I would be pretty much kind and open most of the time, while managing to set up fairly appropriate boundaries, but I was generally reluctant to challenge situations too intensely. At times, however, I would swing to the other side, in which I embraced the 'killer' archetype in confrontation with people and situations. I can see now that there was a link with addictive behaviors as I enjoyed the adrenaline energy of my killer lightning strikes. Now, over time, and after a couple of re-enactments of the old pattern, a middle path has opened up: I am able to lay things on the line if necessary, but with love. Now as action comes from no-self the mood is more a radical intensity than an adrenaline-fuelled outburst. Gone, is the need to reinforce my image and win in any confrontation; without a self there is no longer a desire to prove that I am better than somebody else. In the interconnectedness of existence, these situations involve other beings which are really just parts of the vastness. Yet, there is no single recipe for all situations; there may be a loving restraint or a dynamic assertiveness; or a situation may call for the radiation of an intense abyss energy. If people find such intensity threatening, I invite them to look within—within themselves and within the annihilating darkness—and to sense the loving energy that fuels it. Sometimes I like to describe it as the loving 'black velvet' energy. Love and death are co-mingling in the intensity of the moment in a sublime, mysterious way.

Before we move on to explore in the next chapter the beingness, the isness, of each moment, take a moment to explore your awareness of letting go in relationships.

Exercise 15: **Touch and let go**

✼

In each moment of a relationship, see if you can enjoy it fully, and yet realize that there are no guarantees. This could be the last moment of connection, so you let go of the future.

Notice when you are really enjoying a relationship:

> Celebrate the enjoyment in the moment
>
> Notice how as the moment passes the mind wants to hang on
>
> *See if you can feel the sense of grabbing on to the relationship to guarantee its future*
>
> Notice immediately how this grabbing makes you tense, worried and contracted
>
> *In this moment, realize there is no way now that you can guarantee a future moment*
>
> *Life is dangerous, things may change*
>
> *Notice just how much you are grabbing and hanging on*
>
> *Realize that hanging on is futile, it just makes you miserable*
>
> Let go of your demand
>
> *Feel the relief as you let go of grabbing onto the illusion of a guarantee for the future of the relationship*
>
> *You are free to enjoy whatever the new moment brings*

Chapter 19: Enjoying Just Being

When I see that I am nothing, that is wisdom. When I see that I am everything, that is love. My life is that which moves between the two.

Nisargadatta Maharaj, *I Am That*

In each moment the sense of no-self is crystal clear. I see all that kept me tied into the sense of 'I' was at the bottom of everything an attachment to an 'I' thought—that's all it was, just an 'I' thought. In awareness, the 'I' thought can be just dissolved back to the source. The 'I' thought needs some other objects to grasp onto to keep it alive, and once it is seen in its naked 'I' sense, it easily dissolves by itself. Once this is seen clearly, we can always be vigilant, keep looking inward, and just allow the 'I' thought to dissolve back into the emptiness from whence it came. So now, to keep clear of the 'I', it is just an ongoing process of inquiry such as looking at "Who is having this experience?" In an instant of seeing, the 'I' thought dissolves back to the source.

Abiding in no-self, abiding in the heart of an interconnected beingness, allows the apparent 'me' to come from a place of love. I am not after securing power for the 'I' in each moment or even trying to prop it up in any way. It is in vulnerable insecurity that I embrace existence in each moment, and the magic of existence reveals itself. Even to use the word 'vulnerability' reveals a paradox; it implies the potential to be hurt, but there is no special separate 'me' to be hurt. And now, as I work with people, I see clearly that we are all caught up in the same vulnerable interconnected consciousness energy. Even so, it can happen that we get frightened of this blown-wide-open vulnerability, and try to protect ourselves by using some of the old escapist tricks of our addiction. But, really, it is apparent that there is nothing to be managed in each moment. Like everyone else, I do not have to take care of the self, and can simply stay in the embracement of no-self in the vastness of existence in each moment. Awakening is simply an embracement of not-two in each moment. The clarity of this seeing can make a person laugh in transcendent delight.

There is no longer the woundedness of being a separate self fighting to exist and to survive against all the objects in existence that once we experienced as 'other'. Instead, it feels like this illusion of self body-mind has come home and that home is existence itself. All of this involves an embracement of the divine mystery, a place that we always have been looking for: "to behold the mystery is to be at home".[1] Of course, we have never left that home, but it is as if there was a change of occupancy. There used to be the illusion of the separate independent self, and now nobody, is there but the absolute *what is* of existence. Once upon a time I used to be a somebody, and now there is nobody and yet, paradoxically that nobody is everything and everywhere. So now, in this interconnecting energy, loving beingness flows. Any grasping of the self can be just let go in the moment if it arises, and a return to the full emptiness of existence is made.

It really is just a relaxation into isness or being—this is the ultimate wholeness. Existence is seen to be a pure subjective embrace of consciousness and the whole world is seen to be a modification of consciousness with no independent reality. We are consciousness itself. All of the seeking has been ultimately unnecessary as it is seen that it is all available right here, right now. With the letting go of seeking and giving up of the goal of enlightenment, one has become free to enjoy *what is*. A deep form of relaxation takes place as one sees clearly *this is it*. There is nowhere to go, and nothing to do. True rest is now possible as there is truly nowhere we have to be, no goal other than this. With the disappearance of all goals, the personal self disappears, and there is nobody there to be tense. This moment is enough as it is seen that all moments are the eternal present.

Having given up striving, a deep relaxation takes place as there is no place to go, and nothing to do. Understanding that all is perfect as it is right now means we do not have to strive to change anything or anyone in this place of neither me nor you. Everything is okay in suchness as it is right now. In this isness it is all here, right now. This isness is it. There is no method to let go, it is just a seeing in this moment.

I see all aspects of existence intermingle in the intensity of existence in this moment, and I can lovingly enjoy the cosmic dance and play of existence in each moment. In loving presence, I am free to work with anybody, and not be afraid of another being's negative impact as the need to survive has already been given up. In the choiceless awareness of *what is*, mind's discriminations as to what was seen as negative and what was seen as positive dissolve. Now, as I have nothing to defend, I am free to connect with other beings in a relaxed way. The sense of so-called success and failure dissolves as those concepts relate to a non-existent special 'me'. As I look around I see that the whole of existence is enlightened and I do not need to make distinctions in this cosmic play. I see the vastness of existence available to all beings, and have no concerns about a person's merit or worthiness.

In the moment, I now come from a place of loving beingness. There was a time when I thought I was on the golden path, and the special 'me' was going to be the answer. I had the disease of specialness and grasping at the dream of awakening just like everybody else. Now, I do not need to try to be humble, existence has already humbled me in revealing the illusion of my separate self. I am free to enjoy the interconnectedness of the isness of each moment. Try it for yourself.

Execise 16: **Enjoying just being**

✳

In this moment, see if you can enjoy just being.

Relax into your sense of presence in the moment:

Surrender completely to the moment

Just allow yourself to dissolve into the beingness of this moment

See there is no past, no future, just this moment

Enjoy the pure subjectivity of awareness of this moment

See how everything is contained in the awareness of the moment

See that reality is not-two, there is no self and no other, there are no separate beings

Let your awareness expand to include everything in existence

See how your awareness expands beyond the mountains, the oceans and the sky

Just stay in the isness of the moment

See how your awareness expands so much it approaches infinity

Stay in this isness for the next ten minutes

Enjoy the translucent delight of the isness

GARY TZU

Notice how refreshed you are after ten minutes
All is available through embracing the isness of the moment
This isness is your home
Just being

Chapter 20: Accepting Failurehood and Imperfection

One thing, all things, move among and intermingle, without distinction. To live in this realization is to be without anxiety about non-perfection.

Sosan, 6th century Zen Master

In enjoying the vastness of existence nothing is grabbed onto or clutched at. The ego failed in life, and now there is no requirement to find reinforcements and supports for it to lean on or draw strength from. Now the resulting emptiness has a free run, not snagged by any judgments, with no attitudes of for or against, not seeking support or refuge in anything. Failurehood of the 'me' to go beyond the 'me' has let the 'me' dissolve and now the absolute flows through unobstructed. Now, there has to be a watchfulness that success and its grasping for more and better does not drift back in. In other words, if private goals of one sort or another start forming as a result of awakening, then there has been a reversion to the old success game once again. Success is about to become a failure again.

When one can see that the pathless path is always coming back to a place of total failurehood, it can fill one up with great humor. Any plans of teaching, making a point or an impact, all need to be let go of, and the total failurehood of the situation embraced. So, if we try to make a success out of our awakening, we are regressing. Even the desire to help transform people is a projection into a non-existent future and a way of obtaining success. The grasping nature of this desire delivers us right back to failurehood. Just the other day I saw two spiritual teachers on television announce that they have total spiritual self-confidence, and it was mortifyingly clear to the onlooker that they were trapping themselves—like flies stuck on those old-fashioned flypapers—by an almost gung-ho positivity. As soon as they identify with the concept of spiritual self-confidence, they have something to defend, a persona (in the ancient Greek sense of a mask, or outward appearance) that has to be preserved. Yes, self-confidence may appear to be a by-product of awakening, but what looks like self-confidence is just the ease and joy of resting in no-self with nothing to defend. Even announcing that you are an enlightened person sets up a certain pattern of 'success' that is destined to crash back into failure—as happened with my pursuit of the American Dream.

If we have nothing to hang onto, no 'achievement' to broadcast, then all of existence becomes our playground, because we have taken no fixed stance. We are free to connect with the lowest to the highest, from the darkest hell to the highest heaven. In our nobody state, we have nothing to hang onto—not even our nothingness or our so-called awakening—and no reason to defend against anything 'other'. And as we accept our failurehood in each moment, it leaves us as hollow vessels to let the divine existence keep flowing through us. And much to our delight, we realize it does not take effort to be a failure, it just takes a letting go, so that we are not holding on to anything. We are whole—not just whole in the sense of an integrated psyche, but whole meaning that there is nothing that is 'other', nothing that is alien, nothing that is not part of the existence that flows where it will, that *is* us. Existence passes through 'me' in the moment, and spontaneously gives a lecture, writes a proposal or an article; it's as if the special flavor of existence that goes under the name of Gary permeates and informs each moment and there is a resting in the place of no-self awareness. This is where Lao Tzu's vision of the watercourse way informs us. We can just be like water and flow to the lowest, be okay with being what we once would have called 'useless', and embrace the energy of non-doing. We realize any grasping onto success is a set-up for failure, so we learn to just accept our total failurehood in each moment, and come at life from this humorous and open-hearted let-go place.

Letting go of anxiety about imperfection

Wholeness means seeing "I am not, the whole is." It is not an ideal of perfection but merely a giving away to existence. As Sosan says, "All things move along and intermingle without distinction." Even if I grab onto the mind's judgments about perfection for a moment, I can merely let them go and surrender back into existence.

We can get caught in seeking an absolute ideal of perfection in each moment, and not accepting the perfection of imperfection. Life reveals that perfection needs to be seen as wholeness and not as an ideal. For example, a few years ago, I suddenly met a bear straddling the path on my long distance running trail only a few yards in front of me. As I slowly turned around, I could feel the fear emanating through my body, and the realization that if the bear was in a bad mood or hungry, this could be it. The intense trembling almost instantaneously turned to a vast surreal energy of acceptance in the moment of possible death. As I began to run away from the bear, I knew that these might be my final moments of embodiment. As I ran, there was a vast surreal transcendent delight energy running through me. I paused after running hard for ten minutes, and looked back and saw no bear in sight. I stopped and enjoyed the peaceful sublimity of the moment. I had totally enjoyed the imperfection of the vast outburst of fear in encountering the bear. It was perfect!

Recently, in a decision-making meeting, I began selling a new graduate program in addictions and mental health counseling to my senior administrators at the university. I paused after a few sentences and noticed the intense abyss energy in the room, so alive that I was almost rendered speechless. Nobody else seemed to notice. Rather than judging this annihilating awesome energy of the abyss, I waited for a few moments and continued speaking. It felt like the ocean of existence was speaking through me. I was swept away in the one vast interconnected energy and the words that I used seemed to flow through the rest of the group easily. I entertained their questions, and some of their objections to the new program. I enjoyed the transcendent coolness and delight of the situation. In moments like this, the abyss is so intense that all is subsumed in its formless wildness.

So-called imperfection can show up in small ways. The body feels tired, almost exhausted, at the end of a day teaching at the university. I make no judgments about this, as I understand that this is the way it goes. As I spent some quiet time in my room later, I noticed how underneath the tired body is a vast refreshing energy of existence in which there is rest and deep refreshment.

I have been lecturing for an hour and a half, and notice now my pronunciation of words is starting to slip. I start to stumble a little bit, and I realized that it is time to wrap up the lecture. I accept this is the way it is, I can give a dynamic talk but reach my limits after about an hour and a half. Nothing can be done. If I try to push on too much further in my tiredness, I get word salad. So, I smile to myself, and announce a break to the class. To me, it is just a giving up of the addictive dream of perfection and its accompanying non-stop grinding towards some ideal in which the present state is never good enough.

Even the ideal of helping or having an impact has to be let go of. I looked over at my client in the group and summarized her dilemma. I said to her, "It is like you don't see that it is your own mind that is finishing you off, not your work situation." She looked over at me, very puzzled, and said, "I do not get that at all." I looked back over at her and smiled. I was okay with her not seeing that it was her own choices and the preferences of her mind that were bringing her so much misery and suffering in the situation.

I scanned the room looking at the fifty faces, and made my final point, "Sudden change in the moment, known as quantum change, happens when you realize after a long journey of seeking the answer to your dilemma, that after all your efforts and techniques have failed miserably, there is no answer for you. And in the moment you give up trying to save yourself as you realize it is absolutely hopeless. Nothing can be done, and you just stop." [1] I looked around the room, five or six people had lit up in understanding, the others had strange befuddled looks about them, as if they had no idea what I meant. I concluded the lecture before the scheduled break with the suggestion that when we met after the break we did an optional meditation to explore this point of sudden or quantum change even further. The room emptied. I smiled to myself, how delighted I was to have some people to share this meditation with. I felt relaxed and accepting of the people who were going to pass on the meditation, as they were doing what they needed to be doing to take care of themselves in the moment.

This acceptance of imperfection in the moment can even extend to moments of non-acceptance of imperfection. When I can see in the moment a certain non-acceptance of *what is*, I can laugh to myself and accept my non-acceptance in the moment, and it dissolves by itself. Accepting inattentiveness or non-acceptance brings us back to acceptance and choiceless awareness in the moment.

I can be relaxed in each moment if, rather than pursuing the ideal of perfection, I enjoy the interconnected suchness of the present. Anxiety about the moment always involves some form of separation in which I have inadvertently grasped onto the separate self ego again by the back door, and I can laughingly just let go, and once again accept the death of my separate self as I see in this moment it is not even there. A little moment of grasping is just a reminder to let go of self and surrender to the whole. Let myself dissolve completely into the whole. We cannot control our thoughts; we just do not have to believe in them. So, even when a grasping thought comes into our awareness, we can remember it is just mind, and let it go. In this way, we do not have to be frightened of what shows up in the mind in this moment or the future, we can let it go, let it pass through without sticking.

Sometimes, imperfection can even be quite hilarious. In the middle of giving a talk, when I am flying along, I can get a blast of a thought, "What a bunch of bullshit". It can catch me off guard for a second, I wonder where it came from, my own mind or projected as thought energy by somebody in the audience? Either way, it does not matter, as in the moment I just remember it is mind, and let it go. Likewise, when an audience member gets up in the middle of my talking and leaves right in front of me, my mind wants to jump in and make something of it, "Why are you leaving? What's wrong?" the mind wants to ask. But before my mind even has a chance to start grasping I say to it "Who cares?" And all of these thoughts are let go, so I can return to enjoying the intensity of the moment. Any thought can show up, but thought does not have to be believed and held onto.

To be relaxed and sublimely enjoying each moment, I

accept limitations—but the word 'limitations' might better be described as 'different expressions of existence'. The cosmos flows through me in a certain way. I can be vulnerable, open and present, but I am more of a ragged glory type of person in that I am not smooth and refined and sophisticated, but a flowing rough diamond in the moment. If I try to be something else, then there is trouble for me. I accept my own nature. Rather than holding onto the illusion of ideal perfection, I am open to grace so I can let existence flow through me.

It is like Lao Tzu's idea of accepting both wisdom and folly, sage and fool. I can't have one side without the other. I realize that in coming to this place of embracing no knowing, much knowledge has been discarded and left behind. So at times, my no knowing may look more like ignorance, but I am okay with that. My appreciation of my uselessness to others may look more like the path of being lazy, but what can I do? I enjoy doing nothing in the moment as I realize that there is no place to go, nothing to do, nothing to know, and the invitation is to just enjoy the vast sublime beautiful mystery of existence in this moment.

Now for yourself, try exploring the beauty of the invitation to accept failurehood.

Exercise 17: Accepting failurehood in day to day life

※

Having already discovered the total failurehood of your separate self, see if you can apply this understanding in your day to day life.

> Think of a situation in your life where you have been trying to be a success:
>
> Be aware of how tense you have become
>
> *It is like the wave of the ocean is trying to have a separate destiny*
>
> Laugh to yourself as you have been trying to succeed and be the answer
>
> *Realize once again success has turned to failurehood*
>
> In this moment, give up trying to succeed
>
> *See how relaxed you now are*
>
> *See you have not actually lost anything but your grasping at success and your tension*
>
> Stay in this relaxed place of failurehood
>
> Do what comes up naturally in each moment
>
> *Realize you can still attend to things as needed*
>
> *Life keeps returning you to failurehood*
>
> *It is the nature of things*
>
> *The wave surrenders to the ocean*

Chapter 21: Embracing Ordinariness

Barefooted and naked of breast, I mingle with people of the world.
My clothes are ragged and dust-laden, and I am ever blissful.
I use no magic to extend my life;
Now, before me, the dead trees become alive.

Kakuan, *The Ten Bulls of Zen*

The old idealized transference game of the special "enlightened guy" no longer serves us in our movement towards wholeness. This book is about the journey from addiction to non-dual awakening, but paradoxically it is also about the ordinariness of it, and how it is available to everyone: we already live in an enlightened existence. It seems obvious that "nobody becomes enlightened" as, by the time a being approaches awakening, there is nobody there. At the end of the journey, all concepts of self, of ego, of an 'I', of attachment, have been let go, so emptiness has free rein, and we realize we are just this vastness of existence with nothing in particular to hang onto. Even our bodies will be in existence just for a short time, and then fall to the ground as leaves fall from the tree. Our minds are just collections of thoughts, which are not *our* thoughts. In letting go, in that detachment from mind, stillness arrives, and there is no way in particular that we can define ourselves, just an embracement of this vast wondrously immaculately mysterious existence in the moment.

It seems strange to make claims about the enlightenment of beings, who in reality are dissolved into existence and long ago have lost their independent separate self-existences. Yet, over time a common pattern is for spiritual teachers to claim enlightenment in some sort of individual way. Some even have made wildly megalomaniacal claims about their special enlightened status. For example, Adi Da claimed that he was the awakened heart master of existence for all of time. It seems laughable and obvious with awakening that there is no such thing as "the enlightened guy". As Jeff Foster confessed, the whole concept of an individual becoming enlightened is a concept he had originally hung onto, but he could now see how divisive that was as it split him off from the rest of existence. It was as if he was enlightened and the rest of existence was not, which was certainly not true.[1] It would be closer to the truth to say that all of us live an already enlightened existence, just that some beings have not realized that yet.

The paradox of letting go of some sort of individualized enlightenment is that all specialness and individual experience is dissolved. One is just existence itself, coming back into the community. It is like the sequence in Kakuan's Ten Bulls of Zen where the man who has chased the bull of enlightenment comes back and in a celebratory, but completely ordinary, way embraces the marketplace.[2] If all of existence has become enlightened with our awakening, no part of existence needs to be shunned. All aspects of life, including Kakuan's marketplace, can be embraced and celebrated. The sacred and the profane are no longer different as each part of existence is a sacred microcosm of the sacred whole. We can share the ecstasy of awakened existence equally in the marketplace or in family life and intimate relationships. If an awakening cannot withstand the demands of an intimate relationship, this does not really sound like much of an awakening. As Ram Dass said, "'If you think you're enlightened go spend a week with your family."

As we drop any pretensions to an elevated position of enlightenment, not only do we become much more open to intimate relationships, but our relationship to life changes as well. As any claim to special awakening is dropped, life becomes delightfully ordinary. There is no longer any special status to claim, and all of life is embraced in a friendly way. We are not the special one, just a friendly being in existence, living in the vast suchness of existence, open and vulnerable to life. But now we are free to bring our joy and passion into the world.

As we embrace our awakening, we realize that awakening has not been a movement away from life, but a movement to embrace all levels of existence. We realize that being caretakers of the earth is a spontaneous moment-to-moment sharing of love. It is natural process of love. We bring that love into all connections, our families, our relationships, our friendships, our careers, our institutions. Our awakening has become ordinary, and something we are willing to relaxedly share with the world. The sacred and the profane have become one.

Dropping special language

In embracing ordinariness, it soon becomes obvious that the way we use language is a very big deal. As postmodernist philosophy has emphasized, the use of language and discourses conceals desires and assumptions that require examination. It has been my experience that much of spiritual language, even non-dual language, can be so exceedingly obscure, mystifying and incomprehensible that an ordinary person can feel like they do not know what is going on at all. The non-dual teacher can actually create more distance from the people he or she is working with by using language as a vehicle for a special mystique that promotes separation. It magnifies the gulf between the 'enlightened' teacher and the follower; it tends to increase the dependency and the illusion of how wonderful and above the normal the spiritual teacher is. So, this reinforces the notion that awakening is not available to all, just to a chosen few. Thus, the embracement of non-dual being seems to be further and further away for the ordinary seeker. The special language can also disguise the fact that the teacher may be using obscure spiritual terms to hide ordinariness, humanness and potential shadow issues. I have seen this pattern play out with some very popular spiritual teachers.

I am not a spiritual teacher myself. I do not even like that word 'spiritual' as it has been so bastardized and contorted it really does not mean much anymore. In my work with students, clients and people in general, I try to use language that makes what I am talking about accessible, while at the same time not give up what I am pointing to. I do not try to dumb it down, but I just try to use ordinary language. Also, sometimes, rather than spiritual terms and language, I use psychological terms to explain the same thing, as we have a culture now that easily understands these. In this way, I do not have to deal with religious conditioning if someone was raised a Catholic, or a Buddhist, or a Hindu. It makes what is pointed at accessible without all the trappings of religious or spiritual dogma.

Furthermore, the use of ordinary language does not allow for prevarications and hiding behind fancy spiritual concepts. The best example I can think of is the notion of 'crazy wisdom' that was used at one time by enlightened teachers to explain actions that seemed unexplainable. Crazy wisdom was justified as the teacher was awakened, and everybody else wasn't, so other people could not understand what the teacher was up to. When we deconstruct that term, we see what actually is going on is acquisition of power, sexual or psychological abuse, infecting students with sexually transmitted diseases, using drugs, stockpiling riches, going on rants, all dressed up as so-called crazy wisdom. If we take away the term of crazy wisdom, our eyes are free to see *what is*. Enjoy the ordinariness of *what is* with the awareness exercise below.

Exercise 18: **Enjoying the ordinariness**

✻

In this moment you are invited to enjoy the ordinariness of existence and all that this entails.

Look all around you

See that all of existence is available in this moment

Enjoy existence as it is all here right now

See that it is always available to everybody in each moment

Enjoy the wondrous ordinariness

See that there is no insider's club, as it is available to all

Enjoy this moment

There is nowhere to get to as it is all here right now

See that even awakening is ordinary, it is just a return to the what is *of existence*

Enjoy the beauty of this all, form and formlessness

See how the sacred and profane become one as we celebrate the ordinariness of existence. Ordinary yet wondrous

Open to all

Chapter 22 : Beyond Birth and Death, the Great Mystery

You have to take the last half step from Peace-Awareness-Bliss into the Mystery beyond the mind.

Papaji, The Truth Is

In the eternal present of this moment, we connect with a deathlessness and timelessness. It is not that we become immortal, but we see "nobody comes, and nobody goes." There is no longer anybody here to die. The body drops at physical death, but there is no death of the self, as the self has long ago been deconstructed.

Life mirrors the interconnectedness of life and death. The reality of death can interrupt life at any moment. Rarely does death come announced ahead of time. An owl showed up outside my living room window for four days in the fall a few years back, sitting in a tree all day along despite the howling wind and the shrieking magpies. On the last day, I receive a phone call that my twin brother had died. Not entirely unexpected but at the same time huge in its own way. He died in his sleep after a tumultuous tumble into a mid-life spiral of booze, drugs and escorts, after two decades of over-the-top work as a lawyer. His dying is my dying, we once shared a womb together and his death brings out my whole relationship to death and existence.

What is my whole relationship to death? Death totally accepted can be ecstatic. How does it become a problem?

If there is any clinging to a separate egoic self, death is a problem. And here I am at the funeral home, looking at my brother's body in the casket, and it is obvious that there is nobody there. This is my twin brother's body, and I will soon be in the same state without a physical body. It does not even cause an inward shudder.

As I look at my dead brother, who has rejoined the unmanifest cosmos, the only process is to die to my mind-body right here right now, in each moment. The invitation is for each one of us to live ecstatic lives as we let go and transcend our separate self mind-bodies right here, right now, and make it a living sacrifice. Be already dead, be in a place of ecstasy, having already dropped the attachment to the body. Ramesh Balsekar pointed to this freedom in the Ashtavakra Gita:

If you detach yourself from the identification with the body and remain, relaxed in and as Consciousness, you will, this very moment, be happy, at peace, free from bondage.[1]

Dropping the attachment to the individual body, in a heartbeat I am beyond death, and have joined the eternal unmanifest existence. From this place, I can be unconcerned whether I have a body or not. Either way, I celebrate the vastness of existence, the loving, beautiful, iridescent form and formlessness.

Sometimes we stumble onto these wondrous eternal moments unexpectedly. Miraculously we move in a moment beyond body, existence, life and death to an awesome unfathomable mystery where no answers are needed. Later we may get caught in an addictive cycle of trying to recreate these moments.

Thus, once again, we are reminded that the invitation is for us to become willingly able to die in this moment, to let go of clinging onto any experience. We embrace the art of dying. We let go of our attachment to our body-mind and discover our true nature one moment at a time.

The true panacea for suffering lies in awakening to reality and *what is*, as we realize there is no such thing as a permanent self, as in actuality no one exists. And as one goes deeper into this, one starts to enjoy what has been called the original medicine and that is "never born, never died". We are the pure subjectivity of the vastness of existence that has always been here. In fact, rather than seeing that we are in time, we can see that time is in us. We were here in the beginningless beginning, and are here at the endless end. We are here in the eternal moment for eternity. There is no escape. When we realize there is nowhere to go, we can truly relax. We are one with existence. We are the eternity of existence itself, witnessing the cycles of the creation of manifest existence and its dissolution. And if we take this even further, we can enjoy what Papaji called the ultimate truth, "Nothing ever existed".[2] We are the vast mystery itself, the mystery from which all arises.

A good time to check out our prior position in existence is just as we are awakening in the morning.[3] Once this awareness becomes clear, it is available to us in each moment. The exercise overleaf will help you to see this.

Exercise 19: **Prior to consciousness**

※

As you wake up in the morning, check out your prior position in existence.

Upon awakening and before you become conscious of anything else:

Notice you already exist

See that consciousness happened to you who is already here to experience it

Realize that you are prior to consciousness

Sit in this place prior to consciousness, and enjoy the sense of being beyond time, beyond any appearances, beyond life and death

See that in this place, you are prior to being, oneness, emptiness, and the big bang

You were there at the beginning, the alpha, and will be at the end, the omega

You are always beyond life and death, and manifest existence

Enjoy this place of being prior to everything

Rest here prior to the emergence of the whole world

You are the vast mystery itself from which everything emerges

The bedazzling mystery

Chapter 23: Ah This!

There is a very simple secret to being happy. Just let go of your demand on this moment.

Adyashanti, *Emptiness Dancing*

All of my *desires* for awakening led me somewhere else, to some other moment in time. This was the addictive path of hope, which is really a hopeless pursuit of the future, a future which exists nowhere, and it drops as we see that all we have is this moment. In fact, the whole addictive path can simply be seen as an escape from this moment. Recovery into non-dual being happens with the recognition that dropping our games and motives can only lead to wholeness. We have to see that all the motivations and desires driving us have not worked out. Our hands have remained as empty as ever.

Only through understanding does desire drop. The understanding must hit us that there is nowhere to go. A mind seeking for awakening is a mind not at rest but filled with desire. It is tense and cannot relax or rest in this moment because it is trying to get somewhere. Thus, we need to see that this endless desire for awakening can actually leave a person in a hellish state of contracted desiring for a very long time. It can go on forever because the nature of desiring is that nothing is okay in the present moment. It is always a rejection of the present moment because it posits that this moment is not good enough, but in a future moment everything may be attained and be okay. The day I saw that this desire for enlightenment can go on and on forever was very helpful to me. I saw the hopelessness of pursuing enlightenment. No matter what I was experiencing, it was never good enough, as I had bought into the habit of rejecting this moment for some future moment. To me, this summarized the addict's dilemma, in that this moment is never good enough, and something had to change. So, with this I could see that there was an addiction to the mind that I had to break through; for the mind, the present moment was never good enough.

All that I have is the present moment. But this moment is a mystery, a mystery that is life and existence itself; it has no question and no solution for they are not needed in the mystery of the present moment.

We get trapped into rejecting this moment because we persist in hoping that down the road things will be better and go the way we want, the way we see them in our fantasies. Life is already available, as *what is*, right in front of us, and yet we get caught in always preparing for what might be. This first step of rejecting this moment for something down the road is a turning point, because it shapes our whole journey. This is really the trap of becoming. While we persist in becoming, we cannot *be*. We miss the tremendous gift of the beingness of the present moment. We have not had the insight that the answer can only be in this moment but, instead, our first stance is already a rejection.

Rinzai, a Zen monk, went by a butcher's shop and the customer was saying to the butcher, "Give me the best meat you have." The butcher said, "What nonsense, I never sell anything that is not the best. Here, everything is the best." Hearing this caused a great awakening in Rinzai because he realized with existence in this moment everything is the best. It has actually never been less than the best.

When we chase dreams, we cannot see that in this moment everything is the best. As the mind is like a bottomless-pit begging bowl, nothing is ever good enough and I came to see that I could be chasing awakening with my mind for a very long time, even forever. Seeing the hugeness of this stopped the mind in its tracks and broke through my addiction to the mind. Now, the situation is that nothing needs to change other than the old way of seeing, where the mind says that if I do this and change that everything will be okay in the future. Here, nothing needs to change. And as I rest in this, I feel the vast magical beauty of existence in its extraordinariness and in its ordinariness, as it is available to us all in each moment.

In accepting non-attainment, there is no place to go, and I can just embrace this moment. With this insight, a totally different vision and approach to life arises. It becomes clear that we spent so many years with the wrong approach. We assumed something was wrong, and needed to be fixed. We had to strive to get somewhere else. We have been searching for a lifetime. And the more and more we search, the more desperate we become. As the desperation intensifies, the madness and the misery take over, and we are willing to try almost anything. The hyped-up intensity becomes almost unbearable, but we do not give up; hoping against hope, we still strive for a solution. Then one day, it dawns on us that maybe the whole search is the problem, the whole game of seeking. We have always searched for something more, some bliss and enlightenment, and it has never worked, and left us in perpetual pain and misery. So, all of this striving is the problem. We just need to give up and enjoy *what is*, even if that is unhappiness or unenlightenment or misery in the moment just embrace *what is*. Stop the effort and just enjoy *what is*. Stop striving and just be one with existence in this moment.

With the stopping of effort, and all the trying and striving, we can enjoy effortlessness. We can embrace doing nothing, and now can just enjoy the moment, with no ego ideal to strive towards. And suddenly, we laugh out loud to ourselves, as we notice in the moment that it is all here: the delight of being, the eternal light, the play of existence, and it has been here all the way along. We were just too busy striving to get to an idealized place to notice that we were already in it.

So, it was the striving that made for unhappiness, and as we sit here and now, relaxed in our effortlessness, we can simply enjoy *what is*. It makes us laugh in amazement, and this sounds so crazily like the old Zen stories that we laugh in the ironic recognition that we too are one of the fools that just discovered after so much effort and striving that the enlightened existence was with us all of the time. In this moment, our mind stops its constant strategizing and seeking for solutions; in this moment of stillness everything becomes available to us, as we are still and present. Now suddenly ecstatic happiness just arrives, no more desiring away from this moment; here and now we can see that we are actually in this ecstatic existence in the moment—this is our home. And it is truly extraordinary and also nothing special, because it has not been produced or caused but has been available all the way along, and is everybody's birthright.

Being awake is our natural state of being: utterly here now, alert, awake and radiant. And the wonder of wonders is that as we relax into existence, we realize that we always have been the vastness of existence, we just did not realize it. We have been searching and seeking for what we already are, a true recipe for disaster. The seeker is the sought. And now, for the first time, we actually realize that there is nothing to be done. We are now mature in our being and accept existence as it is. The part has been unnecessarily struggling with the whole, and now, in understanding, we give up the struggle and allow ourselves to relax into the whole. And now we have come to this place of harmonious settlement with the whole. We have dropped our separate desires, which are really just complaints against existence, and embraced our vast no-selfhood existence.

In this moment, we realize there is nowhere to go to, nowhere to grow to, no goal. It is all right here, right now, and this is awakening. Our journey to awakening has been truly a journey from here to here; we just did not realize it at first. We had to go on a long journey to relax into the present moment, which was actually available to us from the get-go. So, our journey has not been about attaining, but losing, losing our knowledge, our goals, our stories, our desires. And now from a no knowing place, we can innocently embrace *what is.*

Ah *this!*

This is it and this is the end of it. There is nobody here, and nobody here to improve anything. There is nothing to grab onto in the freedom of this moment, there is just this.

So, with this realization, we are free to relax and enjoy, with no goal and nowhere to go. And we are no longer frightened at embracing existence in all of its different levels, so we are open to life, love and relationships, totally embracing them and then letting them go at the same time. We can have connections, ways of making money, semblances of careers or vocations, mingle in coffee houses, restaurants, and theatres, all coming from a place of loving presence. We are free to embrace life completely, with all of its possibilities, but to let it all go at the same time; to touch and let go.

As we embrace life and death, they come together and co-mingle in the intensity of the moment. And with that, we move beyond the circle of life and death, to celebrate existence from a place of never born, never died, always been here.

This is it, in this eternal moment, right here, right now, embracing the mystery, "Ah this....!"

References

Chapter 1

1. Earnie Larsen, *Stage II Recovery: Life Beyond Addiction*, San Francisco: Harper Row, 1985.

2. A. R. Bewley, "Addiction and Meta-recovery: Wellness Beyond the Limits of Alcoholics Anonymous", *Alcoholism Treatment Quarterly*, 1993, 10(1): 1–22.

> A.R. Bewley, "Wellness Beyond AA: Testing the Theory of Meta-Recovery", *Alcoholism Treatment Quarterly*, 1995, 13(1): 1–15.
>
> Marian Gilliam. *How Alcoholics Anonymous Failed Me: My Personal Journey to Sobriety Through Self-Empowerment*, New York: William Morrow, 1998.
>
> C. D. Kasl, *Many Roads, One Journey: Moving Beyond the Twelve Steps*, New York: HarperCollins, 1992.
>
> G. Nixon, "Beyond Dry Drunkenness: Facilitating Second Stage Recovery Using Wilber's Spectrum of Consciousness Developmental Model," *Journal of Social Work Practice in the Addictions*, 2005, 5(3): 55-71.
>
> G. Nixon & B. Theriault, "Non-dual Psychotherapy and Second Stage Sexual Addictions Recovery: Transforming 'Master of the Universe' Narcissism into Non-dual Being", *International Journal of Mental Health & Addiction*, 2012, 10(3): 368-385.

3. Tina Tessina, *The Real Thirteenth Step*, Los Angeles: Jeremy P. Tarcher, 1991.

4. G. Nixon & J. Solowoniuk, "Moving Beyond the 12-steps to a Second Stage Recovery: A Phenomenological Inquiry", *Journal of Groups in Addiction & Recovery*, 2008, 3(1-2): 23-46.

5. O.J. Morgan, "Recovery-Sensitive Counseling in the Treatment of Alcoholism," *Alcoholism Treatment Quarterly*, 1995, 13(4), 63-73.

> G. Nixon, "Transforming the Addicted Person's Counterfeit Quest for Wholeness through Three Stage of Recovery: A Wilber Transpersonal Spectrum of Development Clinical Perspective", *International Journal of Mental Health & Addiction*, 2012, 10 (3): 407-427.

6. Ernest Kurtz, "Why AA works? The Intellectual Significance of Alcoholics Anonymous," *Quarterly Journal of Studies on Alcohol*, 1982, 43(1), 38-80.

7. R.J. Solberg, *The Dry Drunk Syndrome*, Minnesota: Hazelden, 1983.

8. Patrick Carnes, *Out of the Shadows: Understanding Sexual Addiction*, Minneapolis: CompCare Publishers, 1983.

> Patrick Carnes, *Don't Call It Love: Recovery from Sexual Addiction*, New York: Bantam Books, 1991.

9. For an outline of Wilber's spectrum of psychological development model used in this book see:

> Ken Wilber, *The Spectrum of Consciousness*, Wheaton: Quest, 1977.

> Ken Wilber, "The Spectrum of Development," *Transformations of Consciousness*, K. Wilber, J. Engler, & D. Brown (eds), Boston: Shambhala, 1986.

Later, Wilber extended his model to include four quadrants, based on interior vs. exterior axis, and an individual vs. plural axis. The resulting four quadrants are: 1) "I" psychological, interior-individual, 2) "we" social-cultural, interior-plural, 3) "It" physical, exterior-individual, 4) "Its" systems, exterior-plural. This resulted in an AQAL approach, all quadrants, all levels. Please consult:

Ken Wilber, *Integral Psychology*, Boston: Shambhala, 2000.

Ken Wilber, *Integral Spirituality*, Boston: Shambhala, 2006.

10. R. Assagiolo, *Psychosynthesis*, New York: Hobbs, Dorman, 1973.

11. See: Adyashanti, *Emptiness Dancing*, Boulder: Sounds True, 2004.

Adyashanti, *The End of Your World*, Boulder: Sounds True, 2008.

12. A.H. Almaas, *The Point of Existence: Transformations of Narcissism in Self-Realization*, Boston: Shambhala, 2001.

A.H. Almaas, *The Inner Journey Home*, Boston: Shambhala, 2004.

A.H. Almaas, *The Unfolding Now: Realizing Your True Nature through the Practice of Presence*, Boston: Shambhala, 2008.

A.H. Almaas, *Inexhaustible Mystery: Diamond Heart Book Five*, Boston: Shambhala, 2011.

Chapter 2

1. William Glasser, *Positive Addiction*, New York: Harper and Row, 1976.

2. For a well laid-out explanation of how different behaviors and addictive rituals affect the brain, see:

David Linden, *The Compass of Pleasure*, New York: Viking, 2011.

3. For a review of mythologist Joseph Campbell's legacy, see R. Segal, *Joseph Campbell: An Introduction*, New York: Penguin Books, 1990.

Chapter 3

1. Miriam Greenspan, *Healing Through the Dark Emotions: The Wisdom of Grief, Fear, and Despair*, Boston: Shambhala, 2003, p. 78.

2. J. Firman & A. Gila, *The Primal Wound. A Transpersonal View of Trauma, Addiction and Growth*, Albany, NY: State University of New York Press, 1997.

3. Gangaji, *The Diamond in Your Pocket: Discovering Your True Radiance*, Boulder: Sounds True, 2005.

4. Stephen Wolinsky, *The Way of the Human: The Quantum Psychology Notebooks Volume 2, The False core and the False Self*, Capitola: Quantum Institute, 1999.

Chapter 4

1. For a practical approach to cognitive therapy, see David Burns, *The Feeling Good Handbook*, New York: Plume, 1990.

2. For a good workbook on shadow issues, see Debbie Ford, *The Dark Side of the Light Chasers: Reclaiming Your Power, Creativity, Brilliance, and Dreams*, New York: Riverhead Books, 1998.

3. The empty chair exercise comes from Gestalt Therapy. For a good explanation of using the empty chair exercise to work with psychological splits, see Gerald Corey, *Theory and Practice of Counseling and Psychotherapy*, Belmont: Brooks/Cole, 2013, Chapter 8.

4. Cited in N. Foster & J. Shoemaker, *The Roaring Stream: A New Zen Reader*, Hopewell, NJ: The Ecco Press, 1996, p. 11.

5. J. Krishnamurti, *The Second Penguin Krishnamurti Reader*, New York: Penguin, 1970, pp. 228-229.

Chapter 5

1. For a good explanation of de-selfing in relationships, see Harriet Lerner, *The Dance of Anger*, New York: Harper & Row, 1985.

Chapter 6

1. A. R. Bewley, "Addiction and Meta-recovery: Wellness Beyond the Limits of Alcoholics Anonymous", *Alcoholism Treatment Quarterly*, 1993, 10(1): 1–22.

> A.R. Bewley, "Wellness Beyond AA: Testing the Theory of Meta-Recovery," *Alcoholism Treatment Quarterly*, 1995, 13(1): 1–15.

2. R. Assagiolo, *Psychosynthesis*, New York: Hobbs, Dorman, 1973.

3. For archetypes applied to addictions and recovery, see: L.S. Leonard, *Witness to the Fire: Creativity and the Veil of Addiction*, Boston: Shamhala, 1989.

For archetypes applied to the healing journey to wholeness, see: Carol Pearson, *Awakening the Heroes Within: Twelve Archetypes to Help Us Find Ourselves and Transform Our World*, New York: Harper/Colllins, 1991.

4. Byron Katie, *Loving What Is: Four Questions That Can Change Your Life*, New York: Harmony Books, 2002.

Chapter 7

1. S. Kierkegaard, *The Concept of Dread*, Princeton: Princeton University Press, 1944.

2. F. Nietzsche, *The Will to Power*, New York: Vintage Books, 1968.

3. J.P. Sartre, *Being and Nothingness*, New York: Philosophical Library, 1953.

4. R. May, *Man's Search for Himself*, New York: Delta, 1953.

V. Frankl, *Man's Search for Meaning*, New York: Washington Square Press, 1963.

I. Yalom, *Existential Psychotherapy*, New York: Basic Books, 1980.

5. K. Nishitani, *Religion and Nothingness*, Berkeley: University of California Press, 1982.

6. M. Heidegger, *Being and Time*, New York: Harper and Row, 1962.

7. I. Yalom, *Existential Psychotherapy*, New York: Basic Books, 1980, p. 33.

8. A.H. Almaas, *The Point of Existence: Transformations of Narcissism in Self-realization*, Boston: Shambhala, 2001, p. 334.

Chapter 8

1. Chogyam Trungpa, *Cutting Through Spiritual Materialism*, Boston: Shambhala, 1973.

Chapter 9

1. Richard Sylvester, *Richard Sylvester interview*. Retrieved November 8, 2009 from: www.richardsylvester.com/page10.html

2. Chogyam Trungpa, *Crazy Wisdom*, Boston: Shambhala, 1991, p. 84.

Chapter 10

1. Cited in B.S. Rajneesh, *The Grass Grows by Itself*, Poona, India; Rajneesh Foundation, 1975, p. 158.

2. Adyashanti, *The End of Your World*, Boulder: Sounds True, 2008, p. 152.

3. Tony Parsons, *As It Is*, Carlsbad: Inner Directions Publishing, 2000, p. 85.

Chapter 11

1. Patrick Carnes, *Don't Call It Love: Recovery From Sexual Addiction*, New York: Bantam Books, 1991, p. 184.

2. See Book 2, Part 3 in A.H. Almaas, *The point of existence: Transformations of Narcissism in Self-realization*, Boston: Shambhala, 2001.

3. A.H. Almaas, *The Point of Existence: Transformations of Narcissism in Self-realization*, Boston: Shambhala, 2001, p. 338

Chapter 12

1. A.H. Almaas, *Inexhaustible Mystery: Diamond Heart Book Five*, Boston: Shambhala, 2011, p. 263.

2. Cited in B.M. Thompson, *The Odyssey of Enlightenment: Rare interviews with Enlightened Teachers of Our Time*, Mt. Shasta: Wisdom Editions, 2002, p. 191.

Chapter 13

1. Tony Parsons, *As It Is*, Inner Directions Publishing, 2000, p. 138.

2. Greg Goode, *Standing as Awareness: The Direct Path*. Salisbury, UK: Non-Duality Press, 2009, p. 10.

Chapter 14

1. Adyashanti, *The End of Your World*, Boulder: Sounds True, 2008.

2. Cited in Osho, *Tantra: The Supreme Understanding*, New Delhi, India: Full Circle, p. 180.

3. Adyashanti, *The End of Your World*, Boulder: Sounds True, 2008, p. 135.

4. Jeff Foster, *An Extraordinary Absence: Liberation in the Midst of a Very Ordinary Life*, Salisbury, UK: Non-Duality Press, 2009, p. 181.

5. Edward Conze (translator), *Buddhist Wisdom Books*, G. Allen & Unwin, 1958.

Chapter 15

1. Miriam Greenspan, *Healing Through the Dark Emotions: The Wisdom of Grief, Fear, and Despair*, Boston: Shambhala, 2003.

2. John Welwood, *Towards a Psychology of Awakening*, Boston: Shambhala, 2002.

3. Adyashanti, *The End of Your World*, Boulder: Sounds True, 2008, p. 142.

4. Byron Katie, *Loving What Is: Four Questions that Can Change Your Life*, New York: Harmony Books, 2002.

5. Jed McKenna, *Spiritual Enlightenment: The Damnedest Thing*, USA: Wise Fool Press, 2002.

6. See Vichar: Self-Inquiry section in H.W.L. Poonja, *The Truth Is*, York Beach: Samuel Weiser, 2000.

Chapter 16

1. Suzanne Segal, *Collision with the Infinite: A Life Beyond the Personal Self*, San Diego: Blue Dove Press, 1996.

2. Jeff Foster, *An Extraordinary Absence: Liberation in the Midst of a Very Ordinary Life*, Salisbury, UK: Non-Duality Press, 2009, p. 199.

3. J. Krishnamurti, *The First and Last Freedom*. New York: Harper & Row, 1954, p. 84.

Chapter 18

1. B.S. Rajneesh, *Zen: The Path of Paradox Vol.1*, Poona, India: Rajneesh Foundation, 1978.

2. Hakim Sanai (D.L. Pendlebury, translator), *The Walled Garden of Truth*, E.P. Dutton, 1974.

Chapter 19

1. A. H. Almaas, *The Inner Journey Home*, Boston: Shambhala, 2004, p. 403.

Chapter 20

1. William Miller & Janet C'de Baca, Quantum Change: When Epiphanies and Sudden Insights Transform Ordinary Lives, New York: Guilford Press, 2001.

Chapter 21

1. Jeff Foster, *An Extraordinary Absence: Liberation in the Midst of a Very Ordinary Life*, Salisbury, UK: Non-Duality Press, 2009.

2. Paul Reps, *Zen Flesh, Zen Bones*, New York: Tuttle, 1957.

Chapter 22

1. Cited in Ramesh Balsekar, *A Duet of One: Ashtavakra Gita Dialogue*, Los Angeles: Advaita Press, 1989, p.16.

2. H.W.L. Poonja, *The Truth Is*, York Beach, Maine: Samuel Weiser, 2000, p. vii.

3. For an easy-to-follow explanation of being prior to consciousness see John Wheeler, *The Light Behind Consciousness: Radical Self-Knowledge and the End of Seeking*, Salisbury, UK: Non-Duality Press, 2008.

Recommended Reading

Addictions Recovery

Patrick Carnes, *Out of the Shadows: Understanding Sexual Addiction*, Minneapolis: CompCare Publishers, 1983.

Patrick Carnes, *Don't Call It Love: Recovery from Sexual Addiction*, New York, NY: Bantam Books, 1991.

Patrick Carnes, *The Betrayal Bond: Breaking Free of Exploitive Relationships*, Deerfield Beach, Florida: Health Communications Inc, 1997.

Patrick Carnes, *Facing the Shadow: Starting Sexual and Relationship Recovery (2nd ed.)*, Carefree, Arizona: Gentle Path Press, 2010.

Tian Dayton, *Trauma and Addiction: Ending the Cycle of Pain Through Emotional Literacy.* Deerfield Beach, Florida: Health Communications Inc, 2000.

Lance Dodes, *The Heart of Addiction: A New Approach to Understanding and Managing Alcoholism and Other Addictive Behaviors*, New York: William Morrow, 2002.

J. Firman & A. Gila, *The Primal Wound: A Transpersonal View of Trauma, Addiction and Growth*, Albany: State University of New York Press, 1997.

Marian Gilliam. *How Alcoholics Anonymous Failed Me: My Personal Journey to Sobriety Through Self-Empowerment*, New York: William Morrow, 1998.

Miriam Greenspan, *Healing Through the Dark Emotions: The Wisdom of Grief, Fear, and Despair*, Boston: Shambhala, 2003.

Christine Grof, *The Thirst for Wholeness: Attachment, Addiction, and the Spiritual Path*, New York: Harper and Row, 1993.

C. D. Kasl, *Many Roads, One Journey: Moving Beyond the Twelve Steps*, New York: HarperCollins, 1992.

Earnie Larsen, *Stage II Recovery: Life Beyond Addiction*, San Francisco: Harper Row, 1985.

Gabor Mate, *In the Realm of Hungry Ghosts: Close Encounters with Addictions*, Toronto, ON: Vintage Canada, 2009.

Stanton Peele, *7 Tools to Beat Addiction*, New York: Three Rivers Press, 2004.

Tina Tessina, *The Real Thirteenth Step*, Los Angeles: Jeremy P. Tarcher, 1991.

Anne Wilson-Schaef, *Escape From Intimacy*, New York: HarperCollins, 1990.

Non-duality

Robert Adams *Silence of the Heart: Dialogues with Robert Adams*, Atlanta, Georgia: Acropolis Books, 1999.

Adyashanti, *Emptiness Dancing*, Boulder, CO: Sounds True, 2004.

Adyashanti, *The End of Your World*, Boulder, CO: Sounds True, 2008.

A.H. Almaas, *The Point of Existence: Transformations of Narcissism in Self-Realization*, Boston: Shambhala, 2001.

A.H. Almaas, *The Inner Journey Home*, Boston: Shambhala, 2004.

A.H. Almaas, *The Unfolding Now: Realizing Your True Nature through the Practice of Presence*, Boston: Shambhala, 2008.

A.H. Almaas, *Inexhaustible Mystery: Diamond Heart Book Five*, Boston: Shambhala, 2011.

Ramesh Balsekar, *A Duet of One: Ashtavakra Gita Dialogue*,

Los Angeles: Advaita Press, 1989.

David Carse, *Perfect Brilliant Stillness: Beyond the Individual Self*, Shelburne, VT: Paragate, 2006.

Jeff Foster, *An Extraordinary Absence: Liberation in the Midst of a Very Ordinary Life*, Salisbury, UK: Non-Duality Press, 2009.

Gangaji, *The Diamond in Your Pocket: Discovering Your True Radiance*, Boulder, CO: Sounds True, 2005.

Greg Goode, *Standing as awareness: The Direct Path*, Salisbury, UK: Non-Duality Press, 2009.

Byron Katie, *Loving What Is: Four Questions That Can Change Your Life*, New York: Harmony Books, 2002.

Byron Katie, *A Thousand Names for Joy*, New York: Three Rivers Press, 2007.

J. Krishnamurti, *The First and Last Freedom*, New York: Harper and Row, 1954.

U.G. Krishnamurti, *The Mystique of Enlightenment*, Boulder, CO: Sentient, 2002.

Jed McKenna, *Spiritual Enlightenment: The Damnedest Thing*, USA: Wise Fool Press, 2002.

Jed McKenna, *Spiritually Incorrect Enlightenment*, USA: Wise Fool Press, 2004.

Nisargadatta Maharaj, *I Am That*, Durham, NC: Acorn Press, 1973.

Tony Parsons, *As It Is: The Open Secret of Spiritual Awakening*, Carlsbad, CA: Inner Directions Publishing, 2000.

Tony Parsons, *All There Is*, UK: Open Secret Publishing, 2003.

H.W.L. Poonja, *The Truth Is*, York Beach, MA: Samuel Weiser, 2000.

H.W.L. Poonja, *Wake Up and Roar* (2nd ed.), Boulder, CO; Sounds True, 2007.

Karl Renz, *The Myth of Enlightenment*, Carlsbad, CA: Inner Directions, 2005.

Suzanne Segal, *A Collision with the Infinite: A Life Beyond the Personal Self*, San Diego, CA: Blue Dove Press, 1996.

Richard Sylvester, *I Hope You Die Soon: Words on Non-Duality*, Salisbury, UK: Non-Duality Press, 2005.

Richard Sylvester, *The Book of No One: Talks and Dialogues on Non-Duality and Liberation*, Salisbury, UK: Non-Duality Press, 2008.

Eckhart Tolle, *The Power of Now: A Guide to Spiritual Enlightenment*, Vancouver, B.C.: Namaste Publishing, 1997.

John Welwood, *Towards a Psychology of Awakening*, Boston: Shambhala, 2002.

John Wheeler, *Awakening to the Natural State*, Salisbury, UK: Non-Duality Press, 2004.

John Wheeler, *The Light Behind Consciousness: Radical Self-Knowledge and the End of Seeking*, Salisbury, UK: Non-Duality Press, 2008.

Ken Wilber, *The Spectrum of Consciousness*, Wheaton, Ill.: Quest, 1977.

Ken Wilber, "The Spectrum of Development", *Transformations of Consciousness*, K. Wilber, J. Engler, & D. Brown (eds.), Boston: Shambhala, 1986.

Ken Wilber, *Integral Psychology*, Boston, MA: Shambhala, 2000.

Ken Wilber, *Integral Spirituality*, Boston, MA: Shambhala, 2006.

Stephen Wolinsky, *The Way of the Human: The Quantum Psychology Notebooks Volume 2, The False Core and the False Self*, Capitola, CA: Quantum, 1999.

Proof

Made in the USA
Charleston, SC
27 February 2014